200 OLD TESTAMENT SINNERS AND SAINTS

TAKE A CHRONOLOGICAL JOURNEY THROUGH
THE LIVES OF 200 INTRIGUING BIBLE
CHARACTERS

BIBLE CHARACTER SKETCHES SERIES

PETER DEHAAN

Library of Congress Control Number: 2024924268

Published by Rock Rooster Books, Grand Rapids, Michigan

ISBNs:

979-8-88809-121-0 (e-book)

979-8-88809-122-7 (paperback)

979-8-88809-123-4 (hardcover)

Credits:

Developmental editor: Kathryn Wilmotte & Julie Harbison

Copyeditor: Robyn Mulder

Cover design: Cassidy Wierks

Author photo: Chelsie Jensen Photography

Series by Peter DeHaan

40-Day Bible Study Series takes a fresh and practical look into Scripture, book by book.

Bible Character Sketches Series celebrates people in Scripture, from the well-known to the obscure.

Holiday Celebration Bible Study Series rejoices in the holidays with Jesus.

Visiting Churches Series takes an in-person look at church practices and traditions to inform and inspire today's followers of Jesus.

Be the first to hear about Peter's new books and receive updates at PeterDeHaan.com/updates.

CONTENTS

MOSES AND THE LAW

DAVID, A MAN AFTER GOD'S OWN HEART

DANIEL, PROPHET AND DREAM INTERPRETER

CELEBRATE OLD TESTAMENT CHARACTERS

S ome Christians dismiss the Old Testament. They argue that since Jesus came to fulfill the Law and the Prophets (Matthew 5:17), that it doesn't matter. Others embrace the Old Testament, quoting 2 Timothy 3:16 that all Scripture—both the Old and New Testaments—has merit.

We should therefore embrace the Old Testament to inform our understanding of the New Testament, and the faith practices it reveals, through the foundation the Old Testament provides.

From this perspective, we can celebrate the Old Testament. First, it reveals God to us. Second, it anticipates the coming Savior, Jesus.

In the Old Testament a mind-numbing list of things to do and not do confronts us. Yet everyone falls short. We all miss the mark (James 2:10).

Yet the Old Testament also gives us hope of the coming Savior who will offer a better way for us to approach God. It's believing in Jesus and following him as his disciple. This is so much better than a bunch of impossible-to-keep rules.

In this way, we can best read and understand the Old Testament as it anticipates and points us toward Jesus.

One way to do this is to explore two hundred Old Testament characters. We'll cover them in approximate chronological order, given that many of their stories overlap and others are hard to place on the biblical timeline. To provide perspective, we'll anchor our exploration of these people around five notable Old Testament characters: Adam, Abraham, Moses, David, and Daniel.

Some of these two hundred characters provide examples to follow. We'll call them saints, even though they're less than perfect. Others are a colorful list of screwups (sinners), the people who fall short and make a mess of things.

As we consider these individuals on a continuum from mostly good to mostly bad, remember that all of them miss the mark of meeting God's Old Testament expectations. This points us to God's better way through Jesus as revealed in the New Testament.

May these Old Testament sinners and saints point us to Jesus, to follow him and become his disciples.

How do you view the Old Testament? Who are some of your favorite Old Testament characters? Why?

[Discover more about the Old Testament Scripture in Acts 17:11.]

ADAM AND EVE

Our story begins at creation, where God created man and woman in his own image. From them, all humanity follows. After beginning with creation's first couple and their family, we'll consider Noah and then Job, preparing us to move into the second section about Father Abraham and his family.

1. ADAM

The first person we encounter in the Bible is Adam. And the first couple we see is Adam and Eve. Though we usually think of them as a pair, let's for a moment look at just Adam.

In the beginning, God creates us in his image, male and female. This means that Adam, as the first person, exists in God's image. So do we. Think about that.

God places Adam in the garden of Eden. It's an idyllic paradise, yet it's not an idle existence. That would be boring. Instead, God gives Adam work to do. He's to care for God's garden. By extension, we, too, should care for God's garden—his creation—today.

Yet Adam is also alone.

God, who exists in community—as Father, Son, and Holy Spirit —knows the importance of Adam having someone to spend time with, someone to journey with through life. So God creates Eve— also made in his image—as a counterpart to Adam.

Though many versions of the Bible refer to Eve as Adam's helper, I appreciate the translations which use words such as "part- ner," "companion," "complement," and "counterpart." In these we see a matched pair, equal to each other.

God gives Adam and Eve one rule: to not eat from one tree. All the rest of the garden's produce is for them to enjoy, all except for this one plant. This is because its fruit contains special power. It possesses the ability for the people who eat it to know right from wrong, to discern between good and evil.

One simple rule.

Yet Adam and Eve do the one thing God told them not to do. Enticed by the crafty serpent, they eat from the one tree—the only tree—God instructed them to not touch. Yet the ripened produce looks so good. Eve picks some and eats it. She gives some to Adam. They both eat the forbidden fruit.

When God confronts Adam, he blames Eve. Eve in turn blames the serpent. Yet each played a role, and God punishes all three.

Scripture later holds Adam accountable—mostly. It is through him that sin entered our world. It's because of him that we face death.

And this is where Jesus comes in. Because of Adam's sin we will die. Because of Jesus's sacrifice we can live.

Who do we blame more in this story, Adam, Eve, or the serpent? Does it matter whose fault it is?

[Read about Adam in Genesis 2–3. Discover more in 1 Corinthians 15:22.]

Do you believe you can live because of Jesus? Do you have eternal life through him? (See John 3:14–17 for details.)

2. EVE

Eve is a well-known biblical figure. Surprisingly, she's only mentioned by name four times in the Bible, twice in Genesis and twice in the New Testament. Her name may mean "living," and we see her as the mother of humanity, with all future generations coming from her. But Eve is best known for picking the fruit God specifically prohibited and giving some to her husband. As a result of their sin, God expels them from the garden of Eden.

Though most of Scripture places the blame on Adam's shoulders, in one place Paul does implicate Eve (2 Corinthians 11:3), though we must be careful to not take this verse out of context.

Despite this, Eve often receives the harshest criticism for disobeying God. Adam, however, is equally guilty. He could have—and should have—put a stop to eating the forbidden fruit. He knew better. More contemptible is the serpent, who lied to seduce Eve into disobeying God. Because of their actions, all three—Adam, Eve, and the serpent—suffer consequences, which they pass on to future generations. This includes us.

Eve receives three punishments for her disobedience: pain in childbirth, a desire to control her husband, and him ruling over her.

This suggests that before Adam and Eve messed up, we can assume things would have been the opposite for women: childbirth would have been easy, women would not seek to control their husbands, and men would not try to rule over their wives.

The judgment Eve receives transfers forward to future generations, with women trying to control men and men wanting to rule women. However, in the beginning there was neither controlling nor ruling. There is equality, with God intending that men and women live as equals.

In marriage, this doesn't mean wives merely helping their husbands but more so functioning as partners, companions, complements, and counterparts to each other.

We'll do well to apply this mindset to all our interactions with others, both male and female.

Do we try to control those around us? Do we let others rule over us? How might God want us to change?

[Read about Eve in Genesis 2:18–4:1. Discover more in 1 Timothy 2:13–14.]

3. CAIN

After Adam and Eve leave the garden of Eden, they have Cain. The Bible doesn't specifically say he's their firstborn, but he is the first of their offspring we read about in Scripture. Eve praises God for his role in this, the miracle of birth.

Later, Eve gives birth to Cain's younger brother, Abel. The boys grow up and begin to work: Cain as a farmer, Abel as a shepherd.

Cain and Abel both give the results of their labors as an offering to God. We don't know why they do this because the Almighty hadn't asked them to. This is well before Moses commands the people to give God offerings and sacrifices. Nevertheless, the boys desire to give back to God.

Perhaps Cain decides to go first, and Abel simply follows his older brother's example.

God accepts Abel's gift but not Cain's. We don't know why.

One thought is that while Cain offered *some* of his crops to God, Abel offered the firstborn from his flock, the best. Another idea is that this foreshadows the law of Moses and ultimately the sacrifice of Jesus, which requires the shedding of blood (Hebrews 9:22). Abel's offering could accomplish this; Cain's could not. Or there may be another explanation we're unaware of.

Regardless, God affirms Abel but not Cain. Imagine giving something to God and having him reject it. We can understand why Cain was angry and upset.

Still, God speaks to Cain and encourages him to do what is right. Sin knocks on Cain's door. It desires to control him. God tells Cain to rule over the temptation.

As you may know, Cain doesn't.

He invites his brother out into the field. There he attacks his younger sibling and kills him. We don't know if Cain intended to murder his brother, but the story does read as though Cain premeditated the attack. The outcome of death may have been deliberate or accidental.

Either way, Abel dies. And Cain is the world's first murderer.

God punishes Cain for his sin and drives him away.

Two brothers. One dead and the other exiled. What a sad outcome for creation's first family.

What can we do to get along better with our brothers and sisters? When we face the temptation to sin, what must we do to control it and not give in to it?

[Read about Cain in Genesis 4:1–24. Discover more in Hebrews 11:4 and 1 John 3:12.]

4. ABEL

H aving discussed Cain, we now know the story of Abel, Adam and Eve's second child. To recap, Abel and Cain give gifts to God. The Almighty accepts Abel's gift but not Cain's. Cain is angry and kills Abel.

Though we can speculate why God approved Abel's offering and not Cain's, we don't know for sure—at least not from the account in Genesis.

The book of Hebrews, however, gives us a clue. One passage outlines the faith of many of the Bible's heroes. Among them we read of Abel.

Hebrews says that by faith Abel offered a better sacrifice than Cain. Furthermore, it says that because of faith, God praised his gift and affirmed Abel as righteous. The implication is that Abel received God's affirmation with a humble spirit and didn't let it go to his head. In short, Abel kept his ego in check.

Though we might expect God to then protect Abel for his note-worthy faith, remember that Cain had the ability to determine his actions. The only way for God to stop Cain would be to take away his free will.

How hard it must've been for God to not intervene and prevent

Cain from killing his brother. Yet it's not in his nature to stop us from doing something we want to do—even if it's something quite terrible. This is a result from living in a sin-filled world.

Though Cain cuts Abel's life short, we can expect Abel's faith brings him into God's presence right away. What a wonderful outcome.

How strong is our faith? Does God commend us for giving him our best, through faith? Do we respond with a faith-driven humility when he affirms us?

[Read about Abel in Genesis 4:1–24. Discover more in Hebrews 11:4.]

5. LAMECH (1)

The Bible lists no genealogy for Abel, so we can guess that he died before he had any children. Scripture focuses on the descendants of Seth but gives a short recitation of Cain's genealogy first (in Genesis 4). We must be careful in reading these names in Cain's line, since two names also appear in Seth's line, though they refer to different men.

Such is the case with Lamech (1). (The other name to be careful with is Enoch. Also, watch out for Methushael, not to be confused with Methuselah.)

We know little about Lamech, but two things stand out.

First, Lamech marries two women, Adah and Zillah.

This is the first time any form of the word *marriage* occurs in the Bible, and this passage is also the first reference to polygamy. Though Bible scholars often place elevated importance on the first time a word appears in Scripture, we must be careful not to connect marriage with polygamy.

The Bible merely states that Lamech married two women, but it adds no commentary. Therefore, we're wrong to take this descriptive text as approval for polygamy or as a warning against it. Notably, this may be the only time in Scripture when a man has multiple wives that doesn't result in conflict or heartache. Consider the multiple wives of Abraham, Jacob, David, Solomon, and many others. Each suffers as a result.

The other thing we know about Lamech is that he kills a man. He's the Bible's second recorded murderer, with Cain being the first.

Though we could charitably ascribe the death of this unnamed man by the hand of Lamech as self-defense, it's more likely an excessive retaliation. Lamech's justification is that the man he killed had wounded and injured him. Regardless, Lamech considers what he did to be less wrong than Cain murdering Abel out of jealousy.

We must note, however, that Lamech's killing of this man occurs prior to God giving Moses the Ten Commandments, which prohibit murder. Yet he should have been instinctively aware that murder is wrong.

When have we responded in an excessive manner to someone who wronged us? Do you think Lamech killed this man or murdered him? What is the difference?

[Read about Lamech in Genesis 4:19–24. All other mentions of Lamech in the Bible refer to Lamech (2), a descendant of Seth.]

6. SETH

The Bible tells us that Adam has many sons and daughters, but it only lists three sons by name. They are Cain, Abel, and Seth.

Most people know about Cain and Abel, with Cain killing Abel out of jealousy. He then flees his family to live in the land of Nod.

As a result, Adam and Eve effectively have no sons. One is dead, and the other is gone. Adam and Eve then have Seth. The meaning of the name Seth may be "granted," for God granted Adam and Eve another child.

He's essentially a replacement for Cain and Abel.

We may be uneasy about the reason for Seth's conception. This could be a positive development, with him being elevated as Adam and Eve's primary heir. Yet the idea that Seth's creation is merely to fill the void left by his murdered brother, Abel, is disconcerting.

Regardless, Seth is born.

Scripture notes that after Seth's birth is when Adam's many sons and daughters are born. Implicitly, this makes Seth Adam and Eve's third child.

The only other things we know about Seth are his descendants. The Bible lists the successive generations as Enosh, then Kenan, followed by Mahalalel, Jared, Enoch, Methuselah, Lamech, and Noah. Therefore, Noah follows Seth by eight generations.

What's even more significant, however, is that Luke lists Seth in the family tree of Jesus. Yes, Jesus descends from Seth.

If the circumstance regarding our conception is less than admirable, do we let it define who we are or do we rise above it? Though we don't know what our descendants will do long after we're gone, how should their potential inform what we do today?

[Read about Seth in Genesis 4:25–26 and Genesis 5:3–8. Discover more in 1 Chronicles 1:1 and Luke 3:38.]

7. ENOCH (2)

As we already noted, Enoch (1) is a descendant of Cain, whereas Enoch (2) is a descendant of Seth.

To give us some historical perspective, here are the world's first nine generations, from Adam to Noah:

Adam,
Seth,
Enosh,
Kenan,
Mahalalel,
Jared,
Enoch,
Methuselah,
Lamech, and
Noah.

As we can see, Enoch is the great-grandfather of Noah, as well as six generations removed from Adam.

Scripture tells us one detail about Enoch, and it's significant.

Enoch does not die.

He walks faithfully with God and is taken up into heaven. We can connect his faithful walk with the fact that he bypasses death and goes directly to eternity.

Enoch is the first person in the Bible to be affirmed for his faithful walk with God. Though it would be wrong to conclude that everyone who walks faithfully with God will skip death, moving directly from physical life on earth to eternal life in heaven, in this case it did happen.

Though Enoch is the first person to experience this, he isn't the last. Later, Elijah will also be taken up into heaven. These two events foreshadow the resurrected body of Jesus ascending into heaven.

What should we do to walk faithfully with God? Why should we want to do this?

[Read about Enoch in Genesis 5:18–24. Discover when Elijah is taken up into heaven in 2 Kings 2:1–11.]

8. METHUSELAH

Methuselah is Enoch's son. Aside from being Noah's grandfather, the other notable fact about Methuselah is that he has the longest recorded life in the Bible, standing at an amazing 969 years. The Bible records many people at that time as living hundreds of years, but Methuselah's life is the longest.

Yet as we move further away from the time of sin entering the world, we see life spans decreasing in length. Death, after all, is the result of sin.

Moses later places a typical person's life at seventy years, even up to eighty (Psalm 90:10). This is despite the fact that he lived to be 120 years old (Deuteronomy 34:7), which God established during the time of Noah (Genesis 6:3).

Accepting the lifespan of Old Testament characters as literal, as I do, we can determine that Methuselah—and his son Lamech (2)— are both born while Adam is still alive. They are also alive when Noah is born. This means that Methuselah and Lamech know both Adam and Noah.

Also, their lives end about the time of the flood. Did they die prior to the flood, or did they drown in the deluge?

Regardless, they were both certainly alive one hundred years earlier when God told Noah to build the ark. At that time God noted the wickedness of humanity and their persistent evil thoughts.

We're left to wonder if this critical assessment of the world's persistent evil includes Methuselah and Lamech. Regardless, Noah found God's favor (Genesis 6:1–8).

What is our view of living a long life? Whether we have days left or decades, what can we do to make every moment count?

[Read about Methuselah in Genesis 5:21–27. Discover more in 1 Chronicles 1:3 and Luke 3:37.]

9. NOAH (1)

Following the biblical story arc, we move forward several generations. Sin entered the world through Adam, found its expression in Cain, and, over the following centuries, chaos prevails. The world becomes corrupt, filled with violence.

God decides to wipe away humanity's rampant evil.

The rest of God's creation can stay, but he decides to do away with people—all except for Noah and his family. The Bible calls Noah righteous. This means he lives rightly, even though God has not yet defined what that means. Noah is blameless in his life and walks faithfully with God.

Scripture doesn't tell us the spiritual condition of Noah's family: his wife, his three sons, and their wives. These seven may be righteous like Noah, but the Bible doesn't say that. Regardless, God plans to save all eight. A better understanding is that they will live not because of their own merit but because of Noah's. So it is with us and Jesus.

God plans to send a massive flood to destroy the world. Only these eight people will survive. Everyone else will die. Most land animals will perish as innocent victims in all this. Then God will allow humanity to start anew, through Noah. It's a massive do-over, Creation 2.0.

To accomplish this, God tells Noah to build an ark, a huge boat, one big enough to carry a representative pair of each species and seven pairs of clean animals—along with enough food for all.

Noah obeys.

People back then lived for several centuries, and it takes Noah and his family one hundred years to complete this massive project. Building an ark doesn't make sense and requires years of back-breaking work. Yet they persist, no doubt enduring the ridicule of those around them and making many sacrifices as they build God's boat, all the while attending to the daily needs of living.

When the rains come and the floodwaters rise, Noah, his family, and the animals God sends to them board the ark. God seals them inside and they survive the great deluge.

When the waters recede, eight people emerge.

God then gives Noah the same command he gave Adam and Eve, to be fruitful and multiply. They do. We're here today as a result.

God told Noah to do something difficult that didn't make sense from a human perspective. But Noah obeyed and saved his family, along with giving humanity a fresh start.

We applaud Noah for his obedience to God.

How well do we do at obeying God? Would we be obedient like Noah if God told us to undertake a huge task that would take several years to complete?

[Read about Noah in Genesis 5:28–9:29. Discover more in Hebrews 11:7.]

10. SHEM

The Bible doesn't tell us the name of Noah's wife, but we do know the names of their three sons: Shem, Ham, and Japheth.

Scripture says Noah obeyed God in building the ark. We can only assume his boys helped. If they didn't, why would God allow them to enter the ark and live?

After the flood, Noah, a farmer, plants a vineyard. He makes some wine, gets drunk, and lounges around without his clothes. Hearing this, Shem and his brother Japheth modestly cover their father, without looking at his nakedness.

When Noah sobers, he blesses Shem and Japheth for their chaste action, specifically elevating Shem over his brothers.

As we read the family tree of Shem, we come across Abram, later called Abraham. Through Shem's lineage we have Father Abraham and, much later, Jesus.

How can we be an example to do what is right? When we see someone doing what's wrong, do we seek to make things better?

[Read about Shem and his brothers in Genesis 9:18–27. Discover Shem's family tree in Genesis 11:10–26.]

11. HAM

Of Noah's three sons, the Bible lists Ham second, even though he is, in fact, the youngest. Scripture only gives us one story about him. It's his role in the account of his father's drunken stupor.

It's Ham who discovers his father inebriated and naked. He could have discreetly covered his dad. He doesn't. Instead, he tells his brothers. Though we don't know Ham's motives, we doubt he seeks their advice on what to do. More likely he approaches them with the glee of a gossip, sharing the tantalizing tidbits of what dear old dad has done. In short, he's laughing at his father and expecting his brothers to join him.

While Ham does nothing to help alleviate his dad's situation and prevent future embarrassment, brothers Shem and Japheth do both.

When Noah sobers and learns what happened, he blesses Shem and Japheth for their proper response but not before cursing Ham. We don't know why, but Noah directs his displeasure at Ham's son Canaan, pronouncing Canaan will be the lowest of slaves to his brothers. And later, while blessing Japheth, Noah specifically proclaims Canaan will be the slave of Japheth. This makes us wonder if Canaan wasn't also involved in his father Ham's folly.

Ham has four sons. In addition to Canaan, he has Cush, Egypt, and Put. From Canaan we have the Canaanites, a recurring irritant to God's chosen people, the Israelites, who descend from Canaan's uncle Shem.

The only other reference we see of Ham occurs in Psalms, where it talks about the tents of Ham and the land of Ham, presumably where some of Ham's descendants settled.

Whether we're the youngest in our family or not, what can we do to rise above our station to act with integrity? When we see someone's misfortune are we quick to tell others about it (gossip) or do we keep it to ourselves?

[Read about Ham and his brothers in Genesis 9:18–27. Discover Ham's family tree in Genesis 10:6–20.]

12. CANAAN

C anaan is the son of Ham and the grandson of Noah. The story of Canaan is perplexing. When Noah's son Ham finds his father drunk, he acts disrespectfully. His two brothers act appropriately.

When Noah discovers what his sons did when he was inebriated, he explicitly blames Ham's son Canaan. This is despite Canaan not having any role in what happened.

We're left to wonder if we don't know the full story or if Noah reached the wrong conclusion. Nevertheless, Noah proclaims curses on Canaan.

This doesn't seem right or fair, but it is what happens.

We later read of the nations that descend from Canaan. He is the father of Sidon and the Hittites, Jebusites, Amorites, Girgashites, Hivites, Arkites, Sinites, Arvadites, Zemarites, and Hamathites.

Although these last five nations receive scant mention in Scripture, the others reoccur.

The Sidonians (descendants of Sidon), show up 14 times.

The Hittites, 36 times.

The Jebusites, 30 times.

The Amorites, 77 times.

The Girgashites, 7 times.

The Hivites, 23 times.

Scripture reveals that these nations rise in opposition to God's chosen people, the Israelites. And this continues throughout much of the Old Testament.

We're left wondering if their opposition is a result of Noah's curse on his grandson. What if Noah had not proclaimed curses on Canaan and his descendants? Might the history in the Old Testament have unfolded differently?

Though Noah proclaimed curses on Canaan, this is not an example for us to follow. Instead, we should embrace the New Testament perspective and not curse others.

How do we respond when we're blamed for something we didn't do? What can we do to rise above any mistakes our parents might have made?

[Read about Canaan in Genesis 9:18–27 and Genesis 10:15–18. Discover more about curses in Luke 6:28, Romans 12:14, and James 3:9–10.]

13. JAPHETH

We've covered Noah's sons Shem and Ham. Now we'll look at the third, Japheth. Of the three boys, the Bible tells us the least about Japheth, though we know that Japheth, along with Shem, acts with integrity to cover his father's drunken nakedness. And we know that Noah blesses Japheth for his action.

That's it.

Though Scripture gives us Japheth's family tree, it's a brief one, shorter than the lists of his brothers' lineage. In scanning the record of Japheth's descendants, no familiar names pop up. As far as the biblical account is concerned, Japheth and his family disappear from its pages.

What can we do to live a life that honors God? What can we do to encourage our descendants to do the same thing and, as a result, preserve our lineage for God's glory?

[Read about Japheth and his brothers in Genesis 9:18–27. Discover Japheth's family tree in Genesis 10:2–5.]

14. NIMROD

Nimrod is the son of Cush, the son of Ham. Since Cush and Canaan are brothers, this means Nimrod is Canaan's nephew.

The biblical text tells us little about Nimrod. What we do know is he's a "mighty hunter before the LORD" (Genesis 10:8–9). Though this is curious wording, we can understand "before the LORD" to mean "in God's sight" or that God noticed Nimrod's hunting prowess. What's unclear is if this is a result of God's blessing on Nimrod or not.

Regardless, Nimrod establishes a kingdom, first in Babylon and then in Assyria, where he builds the city of Nineveh. Do these three locations sound familiar? Babylon appears 299 times in the Bible, Assyria 132 times, and Nineveh, twenty-six times. These mentions are as the enemy of God's chosen people, sometimes representing evil.

Parallel to the offspring of his Uncle Canaan, Babylon and Assyria also oppose God's promised people and the nations of Israel and Judah.

Assyria will later conquer the nation of Israel and deport its people. In this way, Assyria serves as God's instrument of judgment against his rebellious children.

Not learning from this example, Judah will later suffer much the same consequence. Babylon conquers Judah and deports its people too. Unlike Israel, however, some people from Judah will return to the promised land seventy years later and get a second chance. The people of Israel and Judah tested God's patience and eventually received the punishment they deserved.

In what ways do we test God's patience like the nations of Israel and Judah did? How do we react when God gives us a second chance?

[Read about Nimrod in Genesis 10:8–12. Discover more in 2 Kings 25:1–26.]

15. JOB

We don't know when Job lived, but many Bible scholars consider him a contemporary of Abraham. This places Job several generations after Noah in our biblical timeline.

Job lives in the land of Uz. We know four key things about him:

First, he is a righteous man, acting justly in all he does and conducting himself with blame-free confidence. He puts God first and avoids evil.

Next, Job is a family man. He and his wife have ten children, a quiver full (Psalm 127:5), which people see as a sign of God's favor.

Third, Job is concerned for his kids and their future. After they have a party, he offers a burnt offering sacrifice for each one of them to purify them of any sin or careless thought. He wants to help make them right with God.

Last, Job is rich. He owns over 10,000 animals, with a large staff to oversee his herds. He is the wealthiest man in the area and esteemed by all.

As such, Job enjoys an idyllic life of ease with favor from God. Everyone looks up to him, and Job's life seems perfect.

Yet Satan seeks to torment Job. Though God gives Satan

permission to act, God isn't the cause of Job's suffering, Satan is. Don't forget that.

Satan strips away Job's wealth and kills his children. Then Satan attacks Job's health, leaving him clinging to life with an unsupportive wife. But in all this Job remains faithful to God.

Job perseveres through these afflictions and doesn't buckle under his friends' less-than-helpful advice, as we'll see in the following five chapters.

Eventually, God rewards Job for his faithfulness by restoring his health, returning his wealth times two, and giving him ten more children. Job lives another 140 years, celebrating life with his children, grandchildren, great-grandchildren, and great-great-grandchildren.

When unthinkable hardship afflicts us, how can we remain steadfast in our devotion to God? When it seems everyone and everything is against us, will we continue to put God first?

[Read about Job in the book of Job, especially Job 1, 2, and 42. Discover more in Ezekiel 14:13–14 and Ezekiel 9–20.]

Learn even more about Job and his friends in the Bible study *Dear Theophilus Job: 40 Insights About Moving from Despair to Deliverance,* which explores this classic story as a modern-day screenplay.

16. JOB'S WIFE

We don't know the name of Job's wife. She's a minor character in the Bible's account of his life, so we could view her name as unimportant.

Through no fault of Job, Satan attacks him, wiping away his wealth and killing all his children. Next, Satan afflicts Job's health, leaving him in agony. The suffering man wishes he were dead, that he'd never been born. All Job has left is his life, four unsupportive friends, and a wife who harasses him.

As Job struggles to maintain his faith in God and hold on to his righteousness, Job's wife could choose to support him. She should encourage him. Instead, she turns on him. She ridicules his integrity and suggests he just curse God so he can die.

A supportive wife she is not. Her reaction to his pain suggests apathy toward him, even disdain.

At a time when Job seeks comfort and encouragement from those around him, his wife lets him down. She could have—she should have—encouraged him to stand firm in his faith, to not waver or doubt. She doesn't. Instead, she urges him to give up and die.

Despite this, Job doesn't waver. He calls her foolish and does not sin. God spares Job and restores what Satan took from him.

Do we encourage those closest to us when they go through tough times, or do we make things even harder for them? How can we better support those who struggle?

[Read about Job's wife in Job 2:9–10. Discover more about a good wife in Genesis 2:18 and Proverbs 31:10–31.]

17. ELIPHAZ (1)

J ob has three friends, Eliphaz, Bildad, and Zophar, who hear of his plight and come to offer sympathy and comfort. The sight of his suffering appalls them, and they barely recognize their friend. They weep for his condition, tearing their clothes as a sign of mourning, and sprinkling dust on their heads to show their sorrow. They say nothing for several days.

These three men don't appear elsewhere in the Bible, so we know little about them, except for what they say to their struggling friend.

Each takes their turn in offering a series of monologues to Job, but as we'll see, they fall short in offering him sympathy and comfort.

Eliphaz the Temanite is the first to speak. He might go first because he is the oldest. Or the wealthiest. Or the wisest. Or perhaps he's simply bolder than his two friends.

Eliphaz has had a long time to consider what he'll say to Job. Though his words could have offered comfort to his suffering friend, instead they come out as an accusation, judging Job for presumed shortcomings.

Eliphaz doesn't know Job's heart, and he certainly lacks an understanding of God's perspective, but Eliphaz speaks as though he knows both. We might wonder if his critical words are more directed to himself than to Job.

Then his two friends follow him with their own speeches. After hearing them speak, Eliphaz tries a second time. Instead of correcting the errors of his first diatribe, he doubles down. He persists in the notion that the hardship Job endured stands as a confirmation of Job's evil heart and a mark of God's disapproval. But Eliphaz speaks through arrogance and ignorance. His view of God is incomplete, so his conclusions fall short. And when he casts his flawed logic on Job, he inflicts unnecessary pain on his friend.

For his third and final speech, Eliphaz claims our relationship with God is transactional. He assumes that if we behave right, then God will bless us. And if we do what is wrong, God will punish us. Eliphaz sees Job's situation as God's punishment, concluding that Job suffers because of his sins.

Thankfully, this isn't how God treats his people today.

How can we make sure our words help others and don't cause pain? When things go wrong, do we view it as God's punishment, whether on ourselves or on others?

[Read about Eliphaz in Job 4, 15, and 22. Discover more in Job 2:11 and Job 42:7.]

18. BILDAD

The second man in Job's trio of friends is Bildad the Shuhite. Like Eliphaz, Bildad also offers Job three speeches.

In his first oration, Bildad looks at Job's situation and assumes he received what he deserves. Bildad equates right living with God's favor and hardship with sin and God's displeasure. While this certainly can be the case, it isn't absolute, which is hard for many people to accept. It doesn't seem fair.

When he speaks a second time, Bildad assumes he knows the truth and Job is in error, since his life is on track and Job's isn't. Bildad thinks his prosperity gives him the right to speak, and Job's misery requires him to listen. But high status does not make us wise. Though Bildad thinks he has something worthwhile to say, he is wrong. His words shoot forth as arrows, inflicting hurt as well as failing to help.

In his final and shortest speech, Bildad gives Job something to think about. Between worshiping God for who he is and acknowledging we are nothing next to him, Bildad asks, "How can a mere mortal be worthy to stand before the Almighty God?"

From our perspective today we know that by ourselves we can't, but through Jesus we can. Thank you, Jesus.

What can we do to make sure the words we say build people up and don't tear them down? How do we view our relationship with God?

[Read about Bildad in Job 8, 18, and 25. Discover more in Job 2:11 and 42:7.]

19. ZOPHAR

Zophar the Naamathite is the third of Job's friends to speak. But unlike them, he only talks twice. Might he have realized that their words were only causing their friend distress? Could he have concluded that, sometimes, saying nothing is better than saying something?

In his first monologue, Zophar says that Job thinks his beliefs are flawless. Ironically, Zophar acts the same way about his. Like his two friends, Zophar does nothing to offer Job comfort or clarity. Instead, Zophar uses the logic of an incomplete theology to conclude Job is suffering so much because he has sinned.

The second time Zophar speaks, he shares his view that God always punishes the wicked, making them suffer for what they've done. Zophar concludes by saying that Job's deep suffering confirms he's an especially wicked man.

Do we equate suffering with divine punishment? How can we use our words to help people rather than hurt them?

[Read about Zophar in Job 11 and 20. Discover more in Job 2:11 and Job 42:7.]

20. ELIHU (1)

Aside from the three friends Eliphaz, Bildad, and Zophar, we also encounter a fourth man on the scene, Elihu, son of Barakel. The Bible doesn't say if he came with the three others or arrived later. But Scripture does say he defers to them because they're older. He does this as a sign of respect.

Though Elihu only speaks once, his rant is by far the longest.

He starts by responding to Job's claim that though he calls out to God, there's no answer. Elihu says God speaks through dreams, visions, circumstances, and audible words, even through angels. It's up to us to perceive his message. If Job isn't hearing, it must be his fault.

In Elihu's limited understanding of God, he perceives the Almighty as one who fairly administers justice but nothing more. But we're frail people, we do wrong. We sin. If God *only* administers justice, then he must punish us for *all* our mistakes.

As Elihu continues to speak, we see him arrogantly proclaim that he has the knowledge his friends lack. He repeats his view of God's justice and implies Job is receiving the punishment he deserves.

How does God speak to us? Are we open to hear from him regardless of how he reveals himself? Have we accepted the solution Jesus offers as an alternative to the justice we deserve?

[Read about Elihu in Job 32:6–37:24. Discover the opposite of judgment in Matthew 5:7 and Romans 9:14–18.]

21. JOB'S DAUGHTERS

After Satan torments the innocent Job, God restores what the enemy took away.

God doubles Job's wealth and gives him ten more children: seven sons and three daughters. Though the Bible doesn't mention the boys' names, Scripture records the names of Job's daughters: Jemimah, Keziah, and Keren-Happuch. The girls are the most beautiful women in the land.

In mentioning them by name, the Bible honors Job's girls, even at the risk of elevating them over their unnamed brothers. More so, Job goes against the conventional practice of the day, giving his daughters an inheritance along with their brothers. He treats them fairly, as equals.

In doing so, Job reveals both his heart and God's perspective. Given that Job lives in a male-dominated society, his decision to treat his girls as equal to their brothers is even more remarkable. In doing so, Job shows us that just because everyone else does something doesn't mean we should—or that it's right.

How can we better see things as God sees them? What might we do to further God's perspective, even if it means challenging the status quo?

[Read about Job's three daughters in Job 42:13–15. Discover other daughters in Numbers 27:1–11 and Acts 21:8–9.]

FATHER ABRAHAM

Our next group of biblical characters focuses on Abraham and his next two generations, along with their descendants until the time of Moses. They provide the foundation for God's chosen people: the Hebrew race and the nation of Israel. But before we get to Abraham, we need some background first, so we'll start with Terah.

22. TERAH

The Bible tells us that Terah is the eighth generation from Noah's son Shem. So our story picks up a couple of centuries after Noah and the great flood. Terah has three sons, Abram, Nahor (2), and Haran. Haran dies at the start of our story, but not before he has a son, Lot, Terah's grandson and Abram's nephew.

Though the Bible doesn't tell us why, Terah decides to go to Canaan, which is a long journey. He takes with him his son Abram, Abram's wife Sarai, and his grandson Lot. He leaves behind his other son, Nahor, Nahor's wife, and most likely some grandchildren.

Though they head for Canaan, the troop never makes it there. Midway on their trip, Terah aborts his journey. He stops at Harran and settles there instead of Canaan, his original destination.

Terah dies in Harran, leaving Abram, Sarai, and Lot to figure out what to do next.

Traveling to Canaan represented a long journey for Terah and his family. Though we can later infer that God had his hand in this ambitious move, it's only speculation.

What we do know is that Terah had a plan but gave up before he completed it.

Are we known for not following through with our plans? When we say we'll do something, do others have confidence that we'll do it?

[Read about Terah in Genesis 11:24–32. Discover more in Joshua 24:2.]

23. ABRAM/ABRAHAM

While living in Harran, God comes to Abram and tells him to go to the land he will show him. Abram obeys, setting out from Harran when he's seventy-five years old. He takes his wife Sarai and nephew Lot, along with the possessions they acquired while living in Harran. They head for Canaan. The Bible doesn't explicitly state Canaan to be the place God shows him, but we can assume this is the case.

Interestingly, Canaan is where Abram's father Terah had originally headed to when he stopped midjourney to live in Harran instead. This leads us to wonder if God had originally called Terah to Canaan, a mission Abram had to finish after his father failed to complete it.

Upon arriving in Canaan—an act of obedience—Abram's real story begins. His life stands as an inspiring journey with God. It's a faith-filled adventure, with a few hiccups along the way. Yet he perseveres and God esteems his faith.

One of the pivotal junctures in Abram's life occurs when God forms an everlasting covenant with Abram when he is ninety-nine years old. The Almighty affirms Abram's faithful walk with him and calls him blameless. What an astounding affirmation.

God also promises to make him the father of many nations, even though he has no children. At this point, God changes his name from Abram to Abraham. Abram means "exalted father" and Abraham means "father of many." This name change represents an expanded scope, despite Abraham having no offspring—yet.

The phrase "Father Abraham" reflects both his old name and new. It appears several times in both the Old and New Testaments of the Bible.

Another notable aspect of Abraham's life is the idea of God blessing him to bless others. The ultimate form of this blessing comes through Abraham's descendant Jesus, who dies as the once-and-for-all sacrifice to make us right with Father God.

This idea of being blessed to be a blessing to others is a vision we can all follow. God blesses us so we can bless others.

There's much more to share about Abraham's life. We'll cover key aspects in the next several chapters.

Would God esteem us for our faith? How well do we do at blessing others when God blesses us?

[Read about Abram in Genesis 11:26–17:4, and read about Abraham in Genesis 17:5–25:11. Discover more in Acts 3:25, Romans 4:1–3, and James 2:20–24.]

24. NAHOR (2)

There are two men in the Bible named Nahor, and they are related.

Nahor (1) is the *father* of Terah and the grandfather of Abram.

Nahor (2) is the *son* of Terah and brother of Abram and Haran.

Of Terah's three sons, Haran dies early in life, Abram goes to Canaan, and Nahor stays home. We'll circle back to him in a bit.

Terah sets out for Canaan with his nephew Lot (Haran's son), Abram, and Abram's wife Sarai. Yet Terah doesn't complete his journey. He stops midway at Harran. When Terah dies, God calls Abram to complete what his father failed to finish.

Abram, Sarai, and Lot set out for Canaan and reach it.

Much later, Abram and Sarai (then known as Abraham and Sarah) seek a suitable wife for their son Isaac. Abraham sends a trusted servant back to his relatives to find his son a bride.

Once there, Abraham's servant finds Rebekah. She's the sister of Laban, the daughter of Bethuel, and the granddaughter of Nahor—Abraham's brother.

This means that Rebekah is Isaac's first cousin once removed. Though we may shudder at the idea of marrying a close relative,

God has not yet prohibited the practice, so the pair do nothing wrong by marrying.

What is notable is that God guided the servant to find Nahor's family and confirmed that Rebekah was to be Isaac's wife. Rebekah agrees and leaves with the servant.

In all of this, Nahor does nothing to make these events happen, yet without him they wouldn't have occurred.

How might God be working in our lives to bring about his plan? In what ways might we have opposed him or cooperated with him?

[Read about Nahor in Genesis 11:26–27. Discover more in Genesis 24:15–24.]

25. LOT

We don't know how old Lot is when his father dies, but his grandfather, Terah, appears to take him in. We can assume this because when Terah heads out for Canaan, he takes grandson Lot with him, along with son Abram, and daughter-in-law Sarai.

When Terah dies, Abram travels on to Canaan, taking Lot with him. The trio of Abram, Sarai, and Lot travel together, but seeing how Lot's story unfolds, he may have been better off staying behind.

The first glimpse into Lot's character comes after Abram's and Lot's herdsmen fight over grazing land. The pair decide to separate themselves and their flocks. Being the oldest, the choice belongs to Abram, but he lets Lot pick. Lot takes the best land for himself and leaves the subpar area for his uncle.

Later Lot moves to the city of Sodom, which God decides to destroy for their sinfulness. God tells his plan to Abram, now called Abraham. Abraham lobbies God for mercy, but God doesn't waver in his decision. He does, however, provide a rescue for Lot and his family, sending two angels to extract them prior to the city's destruction.

When the angels arrive, the men in the city want to have sex with them. Lot tries to intervene, offering them his daughters instead. What a horrifying decision. What does this teach Lot's daughters about their value? Fortunately for them, the men aren't interested. Lot tries his best to rescue the angels from the men, but the visitors end up rescuing Lot instead.

With time running out, the angels drag Lot, his wife, and their two daughters from the city. As God's destruction falls upon Sodom, Lot's fleeing wife looks back to see what she's leaving behind. She dies instantly.

This leaves Lot with his two daughters. Fearing for their safety, they end up living in a cave. With their biological clocks ticking and no men in sight, the girls conspire to get their father drunk and sleep with him on successive nights. Lot impregnates them both, and they each have boys. This is the last we hear of Lot.

The life of Lot serves as a tale of what to avoid. We see him as a selfish man who lacks integrity and does what's best for himself. He's also a poor father who fails to raise godly daughters, disregarding their purity and diminishing their value. It's no wonder they have no reservation in seducing him to produce children for them.

Do we make self-centered decisions that reveal a lack of integrity? Are we doing all we can to raise godly children and positively influence those around us?

[Read about Lot in Genesis 11:27–14:16 and Genesis 19:1–38. Discover more in 2 Peter 2:4–9.]

26. SARAI/SARAH (1)

The story of Sarai, later called Sarah, intersperses throughout the narrative of Genesis 11–23. She is the first wife of Abraham and is also his half-sister. Though this thought makes us squirm today, at the time—prior to God giving his laws to Moses—a man marrying his half-sister isn't taboo.

Sarah, whose name means *princess*, is most attractive. Abraham worries that would-be suitors will kill him to get her, so he asks her to say she is his sister—which is half true. He even claims this will be an act of love.

She agrees and does so—twice—allowing other men to take her as their wife. Both times God protects her and works out her return to Abraham, but what torment she must go through when they take her away, and Abraham does nothing to stop them.

Although God repeatedly promises Abraham children, Sarah remains barren. She grows impatient waiting for the Almighty to act. Taking God's promise upon herself, she devises a plan for Abraham to have his promised child through her servant, Hagar. It's an ill-conceived idea, and Abraham is foolish for agreeing to take part. As we will see in upcoming chapters, conflict results.

Later God confirms Abraham's chosen child will come from

Sarah. She laughs at this improbable promise, and God criticizes her for it. A year later, the child is born when Sarah is ninety and Abraham is one hundred. They name him Isaac, which means *laughter* or *he laughs*.

Sarah lives another thirty-seven years and dies at age 127.

With God, all things are possible, even a ninety-year-old woman having a baby or living for 127 years.

Have we ever grown tired of waiting for God to act? In our impatience have we ever tried to do things our own way?

[Read about Sarai in Genesis 11:29–31 and Genesis 16:1–6, and read about Sarah in Genesis 17:15–18:15 and 20:1–21:13. Discover more in Hebrews 11:11.]

27. MELCHIZEDEK

The mysterious character of Melchizedek shows up only once in the book of Genesis. There he meets and blesses Abraham after the patriarch defeats Lot's captors and liberates his nephew, the rest of the town, and their possessions. Abraham gives Melchizedek a tenth of the plunder.

Yet this seemingly straightforward story also intrigues.

First, Melchizedek means "king of righteousness." Next, he's a priest of God Most High. This is the Bible's first mention of a priest, so it must be significant. Third is that Salem—his kingdom—means "peace." Interestingly, the city of Salem occurs nowhere else in the Bible except in this passage regarding Melchizedek.

Therefore, we see Melchizedek as a priest and the king of righteousness who rules in peace. We must consult the book of Hebrews in the New Testament for additional insight.

Hebrews states that Melchizedek has no father or mother, no genealogy, and lives eternally without beginning or end. Therefore, he remains a priest forever with a never-ending priesthood. And he resembles the Son of God. His characteristics parallel Jesus. Some think that Melchizedek is, in fact, Jesus or at least he personifies the Messiah.

Though Jesus physically has a mother and a father, spiritually he has no genealogy. He lives eternally with no beginning or end. Through his death and resurrection, he remains a priest forever, in the order of Melchizedek (Psalm 110:4).

Moses institutes the idea of God's people having priests, but it doesn't start with Moses's brother Aaron. Melchizedek is the Bible's first mention of a priest, occurring four centuries earlier. Melchizedek precedes God's priestly line through Aaron.

There's also the tithe, a gift of ten percent. Moses also institutes the practice of the tithe, but Scripture's first mention of giving a tenth occurs here, with Abraham giving ten percent to Melchizedek. Abraham tithes to Melchizedek long before Moses commands it.

Jesus is a priest like Melchizedek, who both precedes and transcends the law of Moses.

What do you think about Melchizedek? How does this passage inform our understanding of priests and tithes?

[Read about Melchizedek in Genesis 14:18–20. Discover more in Hebrews 7:1–17.]

28. HAGAR

Hagar is the Egyptian slave of Sarah (Sarai), likely acquired on Abraham and Sarah's trip to Egypt during a famine. They could have avoided so much pain had they not bought her—or used better judgment afterward. Here's her story.

Sarah has no children, which she blames on God. She's well past her childbearing years. In desperation, she offers her slave, Hagar, to Abraham to make a baby. Sarah reasons she can vicariously have the family God promised her through Hagar.

This is a poor idea on Sarah's part, yet Abraham accepts it without reservation.

Hagar becomes pregnant by Abraham. Though the pair never marry, the Bible later refers to Hagar as Abraham's wife. Being able to give Abraham what Sarah could not, Hagar looks down on Sarah, who blames Abraham for the whole mess. Wanting to avoid conflict, Abraham tells Sarah to deal with the problem herself.

Sarah mistreats Hagar, who runs away. Alone in the desert, God's angel sends Hagar back to Sarah, promising that her descendants will one day be too numerous to count. Hagar obeys God, and soon Ishmael is born.

For the next fourteen years, life with Abraham and Sarah is okay for Hagar and Ishmael, but then Sarah becomes pregnant in her old age and gives birth to Isaac. Now Abraham has two sons from different moms.

Ishmael taunts his younger half-brother, Isaac.

Again, Sarah demands that Abraham fix the problem. This troubles Abraham, but God tells him to do as Sarah requested, for Abraham's legacy will come through Isaac, not Ishmael.

Abraham sends Hagar and Ishmael off with some food and water. When their supplies are gone, they sit down in the wilderness to die.

But God hasn't forgotten them, and he promises Hagar that her son will become a great nation. Then the Lord shows her water.

Hagar is a powerless victim. She has no say over what Abraham and Sarah do to her. Even so, God protects her. He cares for her, and through Ishmael, her descendants are numerous and become a great nation (Genesis 17:20).

What can we do to help the powerless? When we're mistreated, will we trust God with our future?

[Read about Hagar in Genesis 16:1–15 and 21:8–19. Discover more in Galatians 4:21–26.]

29. ISHMAEL (1)

Ishmael is the oldest son of Abraham and Hagar, Sarah's slave. Though this might make Ishmael a slave as well, Abraham treats him as a son. When God promises Abraham that he'll be the father of many nations, he gives Abraham the rite of circumcision. Abraham circumcises Ishmael according to God's command.

When Ishmael is fourteen, Sarah—who is effectively his stepmother—gets pregnant. She gives Abraham his second son, Isaac. This makes Ishmael and Isaac half-brothers.

Ishmael mocks his much younger brother.

This distresses Sarah, who insists Abraham get rid of Hagar and her impudent son. This will ensure that Isaac will not have to share his inheritance with his older half-brother.

This deeply troubles Abraham, who loves Ishmael, his firstborn. But God tells Abraham to not let Sarah's request upset him, to do what she asked. The Lord's promised blessings for Abraham will come through Isaac. Even so, a nation will also come from Ishmael.

The next day Abraham sends Hagar and Ishmael away.

They wander into the desert. With their provisions gone, Hagar sits down and cries. But God comes to her, provides comfort, and shows her water. Like he did with Abraham, God promises Hagar that he will make her son, Ishmael, into a great nation.

The pair survive. Hagar, an Egyptian, gets an Egyptian wife for her son.

Many years later, when Abraham dies, Ishmael and Isaac bury him. This shows his two sons have reconciled. But we don't know if it's just for this moment or a more lasting connection.

Ishmael has twelve sons, who become twelve tribal leaders. This implies the birth of a nation, just as God promised to both Abraham and Hagar. Ishmael dies at the age of 137.

What can we do to reconnect with estranged relatives or former friends? Do we believe God's promises to us will come true?

[Read about Ishmael in Genesis 16:9–17 and 21:8–21. Discover more in Genesis 25:8–10.]

30. ISAAC

Isaac is a child of older parents—much older. His mother, Sarah, is ninety when Isaac is born. And her husband Abraham is one hundred. At this advanced age, it seems impossible to have a child, yet through God all things are possible. From a human standpoint, we call Isaac's arrival a miracle—a miracle conception and a miracle birth.

Though Isaac is Sarah's only son, he has an older half-brother, Ishmael. But Abraham and Sarah send Ishmael and his mother away after Isaac is born.

With Ishmael no longer in the picture, God deems Isaac as Abraham's only son (Genesis 22:2, 12, and 16).

God tells Abraham to do the unthinkable, to sacrifice his boy as a burnt offering. Though this is something other gods demand of their people—and God will later tell Moses that human sacrifice is unacceptable—since God can raise Isaac from the dead, it's not out of the question for God to tell Abraham to kill his son. Even so, it's a horrific request.

Abraham intends to do exactly what God commanded. With the altar built and Isaac bound and lying atop it, Abraham raises his knife to kill his son—his one and only son—the son he dearly loves.

At this point, God stops Abraham from plunging the dagger into his son's chest. It was just a test, and Abraham passed. This proves that though Abraham loves his son much, he loves God even more.

Yet let's not look at this story only from Abraham's perspective but also from young Isaac's. His father is willing to kill him and nearly does.

This isn't something a child would ever forget. Not only would this surely scar Isaac in his relationship with his father, but it could also make him wary of the God behind it.

Would Isaac ever trust his father again? Would Isaac ever be able to trust God? We wouldn't blame Isaac if he turned his back on both his father and God. Yet Isaac sticks around. He doesn't reject his father, and he doesn't reject God. This is a tribute to Isaac's character.

This story serves as an encouragement to us that, regardless of our past, we can rise above it and not let it define who we become. Though things could have happened that we might want to blame on God, we can still trust him with our future and with our life.

Let's take a step back from the story. This isn't the only time the Bible talks about a father sacrificing his one and only son. Centuries later, Father God sacrifices his one and only son, Jesus. In doing so he proves his deep love for us. God wants to save us so we can be in a right relationship with him.

Our Heavenly Father sacrifices his one and only son to serve as the ultimate sacrifice to end all sacrifices for all the things all people have done throughout all time.

It's a gift of eternal life. All we need to do is accept it.

Has God ever asked us to do something that seemed too big or too hard? More importantly, do we follow Jesus, God's sacrificed son, as our Lord and Savior?

[Read about Isaac in Genesis 21–22 and 26–28. Discover more in Genesis 17:19–21 and Hebrews 11:17–19.]

31. ELIEZER (1)

By name, this Eliezer only appears once in the Bible. He is from Damascus and a servant of Abram. We can assume that Eliezer is Abram's lead servant and most esteemed, because Abram is childless at the time and identifies Eliezer as the heir of his estate.

If Abram dies childless, Eliezer will inherit much. Therefore, from a financial standpoint, Eliezer has every reason to hope that Abram never has any children.

Yet Abram (Abraham) and Sarah do at last have a son. His name is Isaac. They want to find a wife for him from their own people. And they send their trusted servant back home to seek one.

We don't know the name of this trusted servant, but it's possible that Abraham tasks his lead servant, Eliezer, with this all-important assignment.

This, of course, is speculation, but it's an interesting consideration.

Regardless, the servant is successful and finds a wife for Isaac. Her name is Rebekah.

How well are we doing at living a trustworthy life? When someone has an all-important assignment, how likely are they to pick us?

[Read about Eliezer in Genesis 15:2–5. Discover more in Genesis 24.]

32. REBEKAH

Rebekah's family line is twisted. She's the daughter-in-law of Abraham and Sarah, as well as their great niece. (She is the daughter of their nephew Bethuel.) As a result, Rebekah's great aunt and uncle also become her in-laws when she marries their son Isaac.

Here's how it happens.

Abraham is adamant that his son Isaac should not marry a local girl. For this reason, he sends his servant back to where he grew up to find a bride for Isaac from among his own people.

God blesses the mission of Abraham's servant, directing him to meet Rebekah and confirming she is the one for Isaac when she offers to water the servant's camels. Rebekah agrees to go with him to marry a man she has never met. This is a tribute to her character.

Though we don't know Rebekah's age, Isaac is forty.

Just like Sarah, her mother-in-law, Rebekah is beautiful. And just like Abraham, Isaac later passes her off as his sister. This is an ill-conceived idea Isaac picked up from his parents.

Another parallel between Rebekah and Sarah is that both were childless for a long time. Rebekah and Isaac try for twenty years to have children. When she finally gets pregnant, she has twins.

Rebekah favors the younger, Jacob, while Isaac favors the older, Esau. Parents shouldn't play favorites. The outcome is never good.

The boys don't get along, likely driven by each parent preferring one son over the other. As a result, the twins live in conflict. When Esau threatens to kill Jacob, Rebekah feigns that she doesn't want Jacob to marry a local girl, hoping Isaac will send him back to their homeland. He does.

Rebekah is a beautiful woman of noble character. But she— along with her husband—isn't the best parent.

May we not repeat her mistakes.

What less-than-ideal character traits have we picked up from our parents? If we have children, are we serving as the best role model we can?

[Read about Rebekah in Genesis 24–27. Discover more in Romans 9:10–13.]

33. DEBORAH (1)

Rebekah agrees to leave her family to travel to a distant land to marry her cousin Isaac. Her family sends her off, along with her nurse. This suggests Rebekah may be quite young at the time and still in need of adult care.

It's interesting to note that although Rebekah decides to leave her family and travel far away, Rebekah's nurse has no choice in the matter. She'll never see her family and friends again.

We later learn the nurse's name is Deborah, but we know nothing more about her or what she does.

The Bible does, however, record Deborah's death. We don't know why, because she seems like an incidental character in the history of God's people. Regardless, it must have been important for God to note her passing in Scripture.

Whether our life receives celebration, becomes a mere footnote in history, or fades from memory, what we do is important to God. And that's what matters most.

Do we do things to get the world's attention? Is God's opinion of us what matters most?

[Read about Deborah in Genesis 35:8. Discover more in Genesis 24:59–61.]

34. ESAU

Esau is the oldest of Isaac and Rebekah's twins. His father loves him, while his mother loves his younger brother, Jacob. Esau, also called Edom, will later become the father of a people called the Edomites.

The Bible records two key stories about Esau, neither of which works out well for him.

Esau grows up to be an accomplished hunter who loves the open country. One day after a long hunting expedition, Esau comes home famished. He smells the stew his younger brother, Jacob, is cooking.

"Quick, give me something to eat," Esau says.

Jacob doesn't. He sees an opportunity to best his older brother. "I'll give you a taste if you sell me your birthright." (A birthright is additional rights given to the firstborn son.)

"I'm starving," Esau replies. "What good is a birthright if I'm dead?"

He pledges his birthright to his brother and Jacob gives him food. Scripture concludes the story by confirming that Esau despised his birthright and the privileges of being the oldest brother.

If Esau is merely hungry when he asks Jacob for food, then selling his birthright as a quick way to fill his belly is indeed foolish.

However, if Esau is dying from hunger, then he may indeed have easily given up his rights as the oldest son so that he may live.

Regardless, Jacob selfishly withholds food from his brother so he might usurp his brother's position as the firstborn.

Our second story of Esau comes much later. Isaac is old and nearing the end of his life. He wants to bless Esau before he dies. But first he asks Esau to hunt some game and prepare his favorite meal for him. Excited, Esau heads out.

Rebekah overhears this and concocts a plan for Jacob, her favorite son, to trick his blind father into giving him the blessing instead of his brother. Her scheme works and Isaac blesses Jacob, thinking he's blessing Esau instead. To accomplish this, Jacob first misleads and then lies to his father.

Esau's incensed when he finds out. Though his father blesses him as well, Isaac has already proclaimed the best blessings on Jacob and has little left for Esau.

Esau begrudges Jacob for taking his birthright and his blessing. Esau's anger simmers. He plans to kill his brother after Isaac dies.

If we struggle with family relationships, what can we do to repair them? How can we better appreciate the family God gave us?

[Read about Esau in Genesis 25:24–34, Genesis 27:1–28:9, and Genesis 32:1–33:17. Discover more in Hebrews 12:16.]

35. JUDITH AND BASEMATH (1)

J udith and Basemath only show up in one passage in the Bible. They are co-wives of Esau. First Esau marries Judith. She's the daughter of a Hittite man named Beeri. Then Esau marries Basemath. She's the daughter of another Hittite man, Elon.

These marriages are a source of grief to Esau's parents, Isaac and Rebekah, but we don't know why.

One explanation is that their son's wives are Hittite women. The Hittites are descendants of Canaan, whom Esau's ancestor Noah cursed. The Hittites present an ongoing opposition to God's people throughout much of the Old Testament.

Another consideration is that Esau's marriages to these two women may have been acts of rebellion against his parents. Marrying someone out of rebellion is never a wise idea. It will surely be a source of grief.

We should note that Esau's parents send his brother, Jacob, to find a wife from their own clan. Yet they don't do the same thing for Esau. His only solution to find a wife is to marry a local woman, which he does—twice. (He also later marries his cousin Mahalath, perhaps trying to appease his parents.)

A final consideration is that their grief stems from the fact that he married multiple women instead of one. After seeing the misery dual wives caused Isaac's father, Abraham, they may hope to spare their son that turmoil.

Regardless of their reasons, Esau's parents grieved over what he did.

What things may we have done out of rebellion against our parents that caused them to grieve? What things may we have done out of rebellion that caused God to grieve?

[Read about Judith and Basemath in Genesis 26:34–35. Discover more about grief in Proverbs 10:1.]

36. LABAN

After Rebekah learns of Esau's intent to kill Jacob—her favorite of the twins—she tells him to flee to his uncle Laban—her brother—to wait there until Esau's anger subsides.

Telling Isaac she doesn't want Jacob to marry a local girl, she gets her husband to agree to send Jacob away, thereby distancing him from Esau and his deadly threats.

Isaac and Rebekah send Jacob to Laban to marry one of his uncle's daughters, his first cousin. Though this makes us uncomfortable today, remember, it isn't until God gives his laws to Moses that he prohibits marrying a close relative.

Jacob heads east and finds his uncle. Laban has two daughters, Leah and Rachel. Jacob falls in love with the younger sister, Rachel, and agrees to work for his uncle for seven years in exchange for her.

The seven years fly by for Jacob, and soon Laban prepares the wedding. But the morning after, Jacob discovers he's married to Leah instead of Rachel. Laban has tricked him, but he defends himself by claiming their tradition holds that the older daughter must marry before the younger one can.

Laban then gives Rachel to Jacob as a second wife, but only if

Jacob will agree to work for his father-in-law for another seven years.

We can sympathize with Jacob because Laban tricked him into marrying a woman he doesn't love and forced him to work an additional seven years to marry the woman he does. Laban doesn't treat Jacob with integrity. Even if Laban intended Leah to marry first, he should've told Jacob this right away and not seven years later when it was too late.

Yet we also realize that Jacob lacked integrity in dealing with his brother and his father. Might Jacob have treated Uncle Laban the same way? This might explain (but not justify) why Laban dealt shrewdly with Jacob.

Jacob then works six more years for Laban. This time his wages are a flock of his own. After twenty years of toiling for his father-in-law, God tells Jacob it's time to return home. Jacob heads out with his wives, many children, and flocks to return to the land God promised to give to Abraham. But he doesn't tell Laban of his plans. He just leaves.

When Laban finds out, he pursues Jacob. He confronts his son-in-law, who justifies his actions by accusing Laban of treating him unfairly and changing his wages ten times. We don't know if Jacob exaggerates this to make his point or not.

Eventually the pair work through their differences, and they part peacefully.

Though it's understandable to be upset when people lie to us, do we behave with integrity in how we deal with them? How do we react when others treat us poorly?

[Read about Laban in Genesis 24:29–51, Genesis 27:41–28:5, Genesis 29:1–29, and Genesis 30:25–31:55. Discover more in Proverbs 11:3 and Titus 2:7–8.]

37. JACOB

When Rebekah sends Jacob away, she promises to send for him when his brother's anger subsides and it's safe for him to return. She never does.

Jacob leaves with his parents' blessing and their instruction to marry one of Laban's daughters. As we learned in the chapter about Laban, Jacob does just that, times two. He marries both of Laban's daughters, Leah and Rachel. He works for his father-in-law a total of twenty years before God tells him to return home.

His trips mark two noteworthy events in his life, one when he leaves home and the other when he returns.

First, when Jacob leaves home to go to Uncle Laban, he stops for the night along the way. He takes a stone and uses it for a pillow. It must have worked because soon he's asleep. That night he has a dream. He sees a stairway stretching between earth and heaven.

Angels travel the stairway and God stands at the top. He says, "I'm the Lord, the God of your grandfather Abraham and your father Isaac. I'll give this land to you and your descendants, making them too numerous to count. Through you and your offspring, all people will be blessed. And I'll be with you wherever you go and bring you back safely to this place."

When Jacob awakes, he takes his stone pillow, tips it upright, and pours oil on it. He pledges to serve God if the Lord will do what he promised.

This is Jacob's first recorded interaction with the Almighty, but it won't be his last.

Now full of confidence, he continues his journey. God blesses his time with Laban, giving him a family and flocks.

Twenty years later, Jacob returns home. Since his mother never sent word it was safe to come back, he has every reason to suspect Esau still intends to kill him.

Yet God says to go, and Jacob goes.

After his parting clash with Laban, Jacob plans for his confrontation with Esau. Then he prays, reminding the Lord of the promise of prosperity made twenty years ago. He asks God to protect him from his brother.

Sending everyone on ahead, Jacob remains alone. That night, a man wrestles with him. Jacob can't prevail, but neither can the man. At dawn, the man touches Jacob's hip and dislocates it. But Jacob refuses to let the man go until he gives him a blessing.

The man's response is cryptic. "I'm changing your name to Israel, for you have struggled with both God and people and have overcome."

Though the Bible doesn't say if this "man" is actually a person, an angel, or some other supernatural manifestation, Jacob believes his nighttime visitor is none other than God, for he says, "I've seen God face to face and am still alive."

Jacob meets Esau, and he's no longer holding a grudge or intent on killing his brother. The two have a peaceful reunion. God holds true to his promise from twenty years prior that he would protect Jacob, and the Lord answers Jacob's prayer for safety.

These two events stand as cornerstones in Jacob's life, with God supernaturally marking his departure and his return. This prepares Jacob for what is next.

What cornerstones has God given to us? Can we see how he has prepared us for what lies ahead?

[Read about Jacob throughout Genesis 27–35, 42, and 46–49. Discover more in Luke 1:29–33.]

38. RACHEL

In the Bible, Rachel's story starts when Jacob's parents send him to find a wife from his mother's family. When Jacob sees Rachel, he cries and kisses her. She's beautiful, and he falls in love.

Though they marry, her dad first pawns off her older sister, Leah, on Jacob. The sisters become co-wives, forever vying for their husband's affections. Rachel, however, remains Jacob's favorite wife.

Though Jacob loves Rachel more than Leah, it's Leah who has children, while Rachel spends years struggling with infertility. Rachel becomes jealous of her sister. Morality aside, this is a practical reason not to have multiple wives, especially ones who are also sisters.

In desperation, Rachel offers her maidservant to Jacob to produce children in her place. Jacob should have known better than to accept this, especially seeing how badly it worked out for his grandmother, Sarah, when she gave Hagar to Abraham to produce a child.

He also should have remembered his father-in-law's parting words to him, with Laban's stern warning to not marry any other women. Though Scripture never says Jacob married Rachel's maidservant, his actions still go against the intent of his father-in-law's wishes.

But there's more.

Later, in a move reminiscent of Esau trading his birthright to Jacob for food, Rachel trades Leah a night with her husband for some mandrakes. (Non-biblical sources say it's a plant believed to have magical powers, possibly including fertility.) Ironically, while Rachel looks to a magical plant to get pregnant, Jacob plants a seed in Leah for another child.

God eventually answers Rachel's prayers for a son, and Joseph is born. Later, Rachel asks God for another boy. Tragically, she dies giving birth to her second son, Benjamin.

Though she is a beautiful woman with a loving husband, Rachel's life is filled with conflict and in wanting what she doesn't have.

Are we happy with what God gives us, or do we desire more? When God doesn't provide what we want, when we want it, do we make poor choices to receive it on our own?

[Read about Rachel in Genesis 29–31 and 35:16–20. Discover more in Ruth 4:11.]

39. LEAH

While Rachel is most attractive, her older sister, Leah, isn't. Jacob wants to marry Rachel, not Leah. But Rachel's father pawns off Leah on Jacob instead. When Jacob protests, he's given Rachel too. Suddenly, the two sisters go from their father's control to competing with one another for their husband's affections.

Jacob loves Rachel but not Leah—though not so much that he won't sleep with her. Because Jacob doesn't love her, God sympathizes with her situation and blesses her with children. First there's Reuben, then Simeon, followed by Levi and Judah.

When childless Rachel offers Jacob her handmaid to make babies in her stead, Leah does the same thing—thereby escalating the competition.

Sometime later Leah gets pregnant again and has Issachar and then Zebulun. She also gives birth to a daughter, Dinah.

After all this, Rachel has Joseph, and much later she dies giving birth to Benjamin. At last, it seems, Leah will no longer need to compete with her sister for Jacob's attention. But the reminder of Rachel forever looms, with Jacob showing favoritism to Rachel's sons, Joseph and Benjamin, over Leah's.

As a poetic footnote to Leah's story, we read that Jacob later asks his family to bury him next to Leah in the family plot. Rachel lies buried alone in another place.

Leah's father gives her in marriage to a man who doesn't want her, but God cares for her, blessing her with many children and a long life.

Whether we're loved or unloved in this world, do we know that God's love for us is unconditional and surpasses what anyone else could offer? When we find ourselves in a competition, how can we best respond in a God-honoring way?

[Read about Leah in Genesis 29:15–30:21 and Genesis 49:29–31. Discover more in Ruth 4:11.]

40. BILHAH

Bilhah and Zilpah aren't familiar names in the Bible, yet their contribution to the nation of Israel is significant.

When Laban's two daughters marry Jacob, their father gives them each a wedding gift: a servant. To his daughter Leah, he gives his servant Zilpah, while to his daughter Rachel, he gives Bilhah. These two servants shouldn't have had a significant role in the Bible, but that's not how their story unfolds. Their lives have a distressing parallel to Hagar who preceded them.

Here's Bilhah's story:

In her desperation to have children, childless Rachel offers her servant, Bilhah, to Jacob to make babies in her place. Her foolish husband agrees, impregnating his wife's servant—twice. As a result, she gives birth to Dan and Naphtali.

In a sad sidenote, Bilhah's stepson Reuben later sleeps with her. Though aware of what happened, Jacob (Israel) does nothing about it. This suggests that both Jacob and Reuben view Bilhah as property more than a person. This isn't God's perspective but man's perversion, which resulted from sin.

Throughout all this, Bilhah has no say in what happens to her.

As a servant, she must obey her mistress. And she's a voiceless victim to her stepson's lust.

But as God often does, he watches out for the underdog, with Bilhah's offspring becoming part of his chosen people. This means that of Jacob's twelve sons, two come from Bilhah, with two of the tribes of Israel descending from her.

Regardless of what happens to us, do we believe God is on our side? How should we respond when people use us as objects and don't treat us as they should?

[Read about Bilhah in Genesis 30:1–8 and Genesis 35:22. Discover Hagar's story in Genesis 16:1–16.]

41. ZILPAH

As we covered in the previous chapter, Bilhah and Zilpah are wedding gifts to Laban's daughters Rachel and Leah.

When childless Rachel, frustrated over Leah's fruitfulness, gives her servant Bilhah to Jacob to produce children, Leah responds by doing the same thing, offering her servant, Zilpah, to sleep with Jacob. Just like Bilhah, Zilpah gets pregnant twice. She gives birth to Gad and Asher.

As a result, these two servants—Bilhah and Zilpah—produce four sons for Jacob. Even though they're not from his two wives, these four sons are included in the twelve boys who eventually become the twelve tribes of Israel.

Zilpah and Bilhah have nothing to say in what happens to them, but their offspring comprise four of Israel's twelve tribes, or one third of the nation.

What should we do when we find ourselves in a situation we have no control over? When others treat us badly, do we maintain our trust in God anyway?

[Read about Zilpah in Genesis 30:9–13. Discover more about trust in Matthew 27:43 and Romans 15:13.]

42. REUBEN

Reuben is the oldest son of Jacob and Leah. We learn more about him through three stories from his life. Each one could stem from the fact that he is the eldest brother.

First, in an account that reveals his negative side, Reuben sleeps with his father's concubine Bilhah. His actions are even more distasteful—as if it were possible—when we consider that Bilhah is also the mother of two of his half-brothers and effectively his stepmom.

We earlier noted that Jacob treated Bilhah as property more than a person. Reuben's attitude toward her mirrors his father's perspective. As the firstborn son, he may have a sense of entitlement to what belongs to his parents. This certainly doesn't justify what he did, but it might explain his mindset. Though Jacob knows what his son did, he takes no action to correct Reuben or protect Bilhah.

Later, we witness another side of Reuben, when he attempts to do what is right and rescue his younger brother Joseph from the hands of their jealous brothers. His brothers want to kill Joseph, but Reuben talks them out of it. His plan is to later rescue Joseph and free him, but this doesn't happen because the brothers sell Joseph to slave traders when Reuben isn't around.

Years later, after Joseph's brothers learn he is still alive, Reuben takes responsibility with his father to guarantee the safe return of his youngest brother Benjamin. We don't know if his motivation is to appease his guilt from failing to prevent his brothers from selling Joseph into slavery, or if he's accepting responsibility as the oldest son to take the lead in resolving a tough situation. It could be a bit of both.

But the important thing is, in these last two examples, Reuben strives to do what is right.

If our past haunts us, do we let it define us or does it motivate us to do better? Jesus forgives our sins, but have we made mistakes we refuse to forgive ourselves for?

[Read about Reuben in Genesis 30:14–16, Genesis 37:21–30, and Genesis 42:18–37. Discover more in Deuteronomy 33:6]

43. SIMEON (1)

S imeon is the second oldest son of Jacob and Leah. The Bible shares two stories about Simeon. The first concerns him and his brother Levi, which we'll cover in the next chapter.

The other story relates to his brother Joseph and occurs about two decades after Joseph's brothers sell him as a slave. Through multiple trials, Joseph has conducted himself well and risen to a place of power in Egypt, where he oversees the distribution of grain during a prolonged famine. Joseph's brothers (minus their youngest brother, Benjamin) go to Egypt to buy grain, so their family won't starve.

Joseph recognizes his brothers, but they don't recognize him. He treats them harshly. This isn't to pay them back for the wrong they did to him, but to test their character. He wants to see if his brothers have changed.

He accuses them of being spies and throws them all in prison for three days. Then he releases nine of them and sends them home with food. But he keeps Simeon locked up.

He warns them sternly to not return without their youngest brother, Benjamin. Though he knows who they are, he claims this is to prove they haven't lied to him and to show they aren't spies. Until they do this, he will not sell them any more grain and Simeon will remain in jail.

The nine brothers return home and tell Jacob what happened. He forbids them to return with Benjamin and secure Simeon's release. Jacob considers Simeon as dead and prohibits Benjamin from going.

When the food they bought is gone, Jacob tells his boys to return to get more. They remind him that they can't unless they return with Benjamin. At last, he relents, and Benjamin joins his nine brothers to go to Egypt to buy food and secure Simeon's release.

When they reach Egypt, Joseph frees Simeon. We'll pick up the conclusion of the story in the chapter about Joseph. Until then, let's consider Simeon's situation.

The Bible doesn't say why Joseph picked Simeon to remain locked up while his brothers go free. It may have been random, it may have been strategic, or it may have been because Simeon and Joseph's relationship was the most strained among the brothers.

We don't know why, but we do know that Simeon languished in prison while his brothers went home to their families, eating the food they had bought and making no effort to return to secure his release. In responding to his father, Judah notes they could've gone to Egypt and returned twice had they not delayed.

Simeon is no doubt counting the days until they come back to rescue him. He knows how long the journey will take. He knows when they should return. That day comes and goes, but he's still in jail. He continues counting. At twice the number of days, he's still there. Surely, he assumes his family has abandoned him to suffer in prison until he dies.

How happy he must've been—although a bit peeved at how long it took—when he's released from jail and reunited with his brothers.

How do we respond when something takes twice as long as we think it should? Do we trust God to be faithful to us even if our family or friends let us down?

[Read about Simeon in Genesis 42:21–36 and Genesis 49:5–7. Discover other men thrown in prison in Luke 3:20, Acts 12:4–9, and Acts 16:16–34.]

44. LEVI (1)

Levi is the third son of Jacob and Leah. Scripture shares only one story about Levi, an account of something he and his brother Simeon do. Their younger sister Dinah, who we'll cover in a few chapters, is raped by Shechem, who then wants to marry her.

When Jacob hears of this, he does nothing, for his sons are out in the fields. However, when news of the tragedy reaches the boys, they rush home and pretend to go along with Shechem's request to wed their sister.

But they insist he undergo circumcision first, along with everyone in the city. The men agree, assuming this will allow them to intermarry with Jacob's family and acquire all their livestock and property.

As the men in town recover from their circumcisions, Levi and Simeon attack them, slaughtering every man to avenge their sister's defilement. Then the other brothers loot the town and carry off the wealth, women, and children.

Although Jacob criticizes Simeon and Levi for their excessive reaction—and the subsequent risk to the entire family should neighboring towns take revenge—the brothers feel justified in avenging their sister's dishonor, despite the risk of retaliation.

Dinah's rape is a serious assault which deserves punishment, but killing the perpetrator and all the men who live in the city is an excessive response, one that far outweighs the crime.

Several centuries later, when Moses gives the people the Law, he says retribution should be an eye for an eye (Exodus 21:23–25). This command is not an encouragement to seek revenge, but a call to avoid excessive retaliation. It's a directive of moderation.

Clearly Levi and Simeon's response to Dinah's rape was excessive and uncalled for. But they didn't have God's Law to guide them; they only had their own sense of justice.

Still, Jacob remembers what his two sons did, and on his deathbed he criticizes the violence they committed. So should we.

Yet despite what Levi did, God sets apart his descendants to serve him in the temple. From among his clan, Aaron and his offspring will serve as priests.

How do we respond when we encounter injustice? Do we react at all, or do we overreach with an excessive response?

[Read about Levi in Genesis 34:24–31 and Genesis 49:5–7. Discover more in Numbers 26:59.]

45. JUDAH

Judah is the fourth of Jacob's sons. His mother is Leah. Judah has three boys: Er, Onan, and Shelah. When Er is old enough, Judah finds a wife for him named Tamar (1).

Er is a wicked man, however, and God kills him. Judah then gives Tamar to his second son, Onan, to produce children with her in his dead brother's stead. Onan doesn't cooperate, however, and God kills him too.

Though the custom is to pass Tamar on to Shelah, Judah doesn't. Instead, he sends her home to live with her parents as a widow until Shelah is older. But this is a ruse.

When Tamar realizes Judah lied to her and has no intention of following through with his promise, she takes drastic action. She covers her face to disguise herself as a prostitute. Not knowing who she is, Judah propositions her, leaving his seal, cord, and staff with her as pledge for future payment. But later his representative can't find her to pay her what Judah promised or retrieve his pledges for compensation.

He sets the whole matter aside. But this doesn't mean it's over.

Three months later he learns his daughter-in-law is pregnant due to an act of prostitution. Judah proclaims judgment on her: execution by stoning for her sin.

In response, she produces his seal, cord, and staff and says the owner of these items is the father. Judah confesses his guilt and declares her as more righteous than he. He doesn't sleep with her again.

Judah does Tamar wrong, first for promising his third son to her and not following through, then for using her as a prostitute, and last for condemning her to die.

When have we made promises we had no intention of keeping? When our sins are exposed, are we quick to admit our guilt?

[Read about Judah in Genesis 37:26–27, Genesis 38:1–26, Genesis 43:1–10, and Genesis 49:8–12. Discover more in Matthew 1:2–3.]

46. TAMAR (1)

Tamar is a victim who takes extreme action to vindicate herself. She's the daughter-in-law of Judah, suffers at his hand, responds with guile, and gets pregnant through him. Talk about a messed-up situation.

We've shared most of her story in the chapter on Judah. There we acknowledged that what Judah did was wrong, but that doesn't mean Tamar is innocent of wrongdoing.

She could have been content to live with her parents as a widow, but she's not. She goes to extreme measures to avenge herself of Judah's mistreatment. To do so, she poses as a prostitute and sleeps with her father-in-law. He impregnates her. As a result, Tamar gives birth to twins: Perez and Zerah.

Judah, Tamar, and Perez are all ancestors of Jesus, and Matthew lists Tamar in Jesus's genealogy. She's one of only four women so honored.

Do two wrongs make a right? When we're victimized, do we respond with God-honoring integrity?

[Read about Tamar in Genesis 38:6–26. Discover more in Ruth 4:12 and Matthew 1:1–3.]

47. DAN

Dan is Jacob's fifth son. His mother is Bilhah, Rachel's servant, who serves as a surrogate mother for her mistress.

When Dan is born, it's not Jacob who names him, or even Bilhah. Rachel gives the boy his name. She says he's proof that God has vindicated her barren condition, having heard her prayers and given her a son—albeit through Bilhah.

The Bible doesn't tell us any more about Dan, but as one of Jacob's (Israel's) twelve sons, one of the twelve tribes of Israel comes from Dan and his line.

How do we respond when someone takes credit for something we did, like Rachel claiming Bilhah's son as her own? If our life seems to go without notice, do we realize we still matter to God?

[Read about Dan in Genesis 30:6 and Genesis 49:16–17. Discover other sons who do little in Exodus 18:3–4.]

48. NAPHTALI

Jacob's sixth son is the second child of Bilhah. Again, just as with his brother Dan, Rachel names Bilhah's boy. She calls him Naphtali.

Rachel's explanation reveals the depth of her motivation. She says she's had a great struggle with her sister, and Naphtali's birth proves she has won. This means Naphtali's conception and birth occur merely so Rachel can one-up her older sister. This stands as a misguided reason to have a baby.

Although the Bible doesn't tell us much about Dan, it mentions even less about Naphtali. Even so, he's one of Jacob's sons, and his descendants become one of the twelve tribes of Israel (Jacob).

Regardless of the circumstances of our birth, are we doing all we can with the life God has given us? If the structure of our family is a bit unusual, how do we treat them?

[Read about Naphtali in Genesis 30:8 and Genesis 49:21. Discover two other women who didn't get along in Philippians 4:2.]

49. GAD (1)

As we've already covered, after Naphtali is born Rachel proclaims that his birth gives her victory over her sister, Leah.

Leah, however, doesn't accept this without a fight. She stoops to her sister's tactics and has Jacob sleep with her handmaid, Zilpah. As a result of this ill-advised union, Gad enters the world. He is Jacob's seventh son and Zilpah's first child.

If things weren't confusing enough already, Gad's arrival makes it even more so. He has six brothers, all half-brothers. Four are from his mother's mistress, Leah. And two are from his mother's counterpart, Bilhah, who is Rachel's servant. This makes one dad, three moms, and seven boys. In case you don't already know, it's going to get even more convoluted.

As with Dan and Naphtali, the birth mother doesn't get to name her son. Being the surrogate child bearer, Zilpah has no say in the matter. Instead, her mistress, Leah, names him, proclaiming her good fortune for his birth. To Leah, Gad represents a competition, with his arrival allowing her to outdo her sister in their misguided rivalry.

The Bible tells us nothing more about Gad. It's easy to dismiss him as a product of two sisters trying to upstage each other. Yet God recognizes his value. Gad takes his place among Jacob's other sons and his offspring become a tribe of Israel.

How do we react when people dismiss us? Do we think God values us regardless of what other people say or do?

[Read about Gad in Genesis 30:11 and Genesis 49:19. Discover another brother dismissed by his family in 1 Samuel 16:1–13.]

50. ASHER

Leah, having four sons of her own and a fifth through her maidservant, Zilpah, isn't satisfied by claiming five sons to her sister's one (who came through Rachel's maidservant).

Leah again gives Zilpah to Jacob to sleep with. Zilpah conceives and gives birth to her second son. Leah says his birth makes her happy. This totals eight boys for Jacob so far.

Like the other three surrogate sons (Dan, Naphtali, and Gad), Scripture tells us little more about Asher, except for one indirect mention in the New Testament.

After Jesus is born, his parents take him to the temple when he is eight days old. There they meet a prophetess named Anna. An eighty-four-year-old widow, Anna spends much of her time in the temple worshiping, fasting, and praying. She approaches Joseph, Mary, and baby Jesus, giving thanks to God for this child who will fulfill the words of the prophets.

Why do we mention Anna in the story about Asher? She's his descendant, a member of his tribe. It's only an estimate, but Anna comes about forty generations after Asher.

This serves as a reminder that we don't know what our future generations may do. They may take noteworthy, God-honoring actions. Or they may not do so well.

Though we can't directly influence what our unknown offspring may or may not do, we can pray for future generations, even though we'll be gone before they arrive. This is hard to do, but it is possible.

More tangibly, we can point our family in the right direction by doing all we can to raise them well, so that they might one day put their faith in Jesus and serve him.

The rest, we'll leave up to God.

How well do we do at praying for our family? What about praying for the descendants who will follow us after we're gone?

[Read about Asher in Genesis 30:13, Genesis 35:26, and Genesis 49:20. Discover more in Luke 2:36–38.]

51. ISSACHAR

Issachar is Jacob's ninth son and Leah's fifth. That's all Scripture tells us about him. But we can imagine what his life might be like.

With eight older brothers—four full brothers and four half-brothers—Issachar arrives to a packed household. We can suspect he receives little attention.

It's easy to see him getting lost.

Issachar does nothing—good or bad—to record for us in Scripture. I'm not sure if we should be relieved or disappointed.

Yet he is one of Jacob's sons, and his descendants become one of Israel's twelve tribes.

How has our birth order affected the attention we receive and how we view ourselves? What should we accept about our circumstances and what should we seek to rise above?

[Read about Issachar in Genesis 30:18, Genesis 35:23, and Genesis 46:13. Discover a man with even more sons in Judges 8:29-31.]

52. ZEBULUN

After Issachar comes Zebulun. If you're keeping track, Zebulun is Jacob's tenth boy and Leah's sixth. If we speculated that Issachar received little attention in his large family, it may be even more true for young Zebulun.

However, Zebulun is Leah's last son. She may treat him as her baby, regardless of how old he becomes.

Just like his older brother, Gad, Zebulun's name does come up again in the Bible in the mention of one of his descendants. Fast forward to the book of Judges. One of the nation's judges is Elon. He comes from the tribe of Zebulun, a direct descendant of Zebulun. Elon leads the nation for a decade.

If we are the youngest or feel like the least in our family (or work or church), have we ever considered how God views us? Do we derive our value from our position in the world or from our right standing with God?

[Read about Zebulun in Genesis 30:20, Genesis 35:23, and Genesis 49:14. Discover more in Judges 12:11–12.]

53. DINAH

Dinah is the only daughter of Jacob and Leah. She is born after Zebulun. Tragically, Shechem, a Hivite prince, rapes her. After his initial act of lust, he falls in love with her, offering to provide whatever her family asks in payment to transact the marriage. He demands his father make this happen.

Jacob doesn't respond to his daughter's rape. We don't know if he's too scared to deal with it or merely waiting for his sons to return.

While her father fails to act, two of Dinah's brothers, Simeon and Levi, do. They retaliate without Jacob's knowledge. After killing Shechem and all the men of the village, they liberate their sister and leave. Was this revenge, a rescue, or both?

After this we hear nothing more about Dinah. Though we know what happened to her and what happened because of her, we know nothing about what she said, did, or thought.

Did she appreciate her brothers for rescuing her? Was she happy they killed Shechem? Or did she have a different outlook? Despite the horrific start to their relationship, could she have accepted being Shechem's wife—or even embraced it? Might she have mourned the death of her new husband?

Though not causing it or asking for it to happen, how might she have felt knowing her brothers massacred all the men of an entire town on her behalf?

How do we respond when others mistreat us? How do we react when others decide our fate without asking our opinion?

[Read about Dinah in Genesis 30:21 and Genesis 34:1–29. Discover a similar tragedy in 2 Samuel 13.]

54. JOSEPH (1)

We've already encountered a bit about Joseph in previous chapters. Joseph is Jacob's eleventh son and Rachel's first. Since Rachel is Jacob's favorite wife, it shouldn't surprise us that her firstborn, Joseph, becomes Jacob's favorite son.

Jacob gives Joseph a brightly-colored coat, which sets him apart from his brothers. He has a dream about his family bowing down to him, which irritates his brothers even more.

Later, Jacob sends Joseph out to check up on his older brothers as they tend to the flocks. They decide to kill him, but Reuben talks them out of it. They throw Joseph into a pit instead, and Reuben secretly plans to rescue him. But before he can, the other brothers sell Joseph as a slave to make some extra money.

Then they fabricate evidence to suggest that wild animals killed Joseph. Jacob mourns the apparent death of his favorite son, and his brothers forget about him—for the most part.

Fast-forward two decades, and we see Joseph's brothers bowing before a ruler in Egypt as they seek to buy grain so they won't starve. They don't know they're bowing before Joseph, just like his dream foresaw. Eventually he reveals himself to them and they reconcile. Then Joseph sends for his entire family to come live in Egypt.

Between these two events in Joseph's life, however, he undergoes difficulties and suffers greatly. Here's a synopsis:

First, the slave traders sell him to Potiphar. Joseph conducts himself well, and Potiphar's household prospers under Joseph's direction. But Potiphar's wife tries to seduce Joseph. He resists but ends up in prison despite his integrity.

There Joseph finds favor with the warden, who puts him in charge of the other prisoners. While incarcerated, Joseph correctly interprets the dreams of two fellow prisoners. As predicted, one is executed and the other freed. Joseph requests that the released prisoner ask Pharaoh to free him. The man doesn't.

But when Pharaoh has a troubling dream, the man remembers Joseph. Joseph interprets the dream and offers wise advice on how to prepare for an upcoming seven-year famine.

In the end, Pharaoh honors Joseph's wisdom by putting him in charge and gives Joseph an Egyptian wife. They have two sons, Manasseh and Ephraim. Unlike his brothers, Joseph doesn't have a tribe named after him. Instead, there are two: the tribe of Manasseh and the tribe of Ephraim.

Do we act like Joseph and hold onto our integrity even if we might face punishment? Regardless of our circumstances, do we always do our best work?

[Read about Joseph throughout Genesis 37 and Genesis 39–50. Discover more in Exodus 13:19, Psalm 105:16–22, Acts 7:9–15, and Hebrews 11:21–22.]

55. BENJAMIN (1)

Jacob's eleven sons and daughter Dinah are all born while he works for his uncle Laban. After twenty years, God sends Jacob and his family back to Canaan. This is where Jacob's twelfth and final son, Benjamin, is born. His arrival marks a bittersweet moment, however, for Jacob's beloved wife Rachel dies during childbirth. In this one moment he gains a son and loses a wife.

This means Benjamin grows up without a mom. Though he effectively has three stepmothers, Scripture doesn't say if any of them attempt to mother him. Bilhah, as Rachel's handmaid, would be the logical choice, continuing to serve her mistress even after her death. But we don't know if she assumes this role or not. Though we can surmise that all three women care for Benjamin's physical needs, we don't know if anyone tries to fill the supportive role of mother.

Though Rachel is gone, sons Joseph and Benjamin live on, embodying her memory to their father. When Joseph's brothers sell Joseph as a slave and convince Jacob he is dead, Jacob coddles Benjamin even more, as the last living connection to Rachel's memory.

Given this, it's understandable that Jacob objects when the Egyptian ruler (later revealed as Joseph) insists the brothers bring Benjamin to Egypt. Nonetheless, Jacob eventually relents, knowing a return trip is necessary to secure the food they need to survive.

Although the Bible tells us much about the older brother, Joseph, it reveals little about the younger brother, Benjamin.

There are, however, three notable people in Scripture who are Benjamin's descendants. One is King Saul, Israel's first ruler (1 Samuel 9:1, 16). The others are Mordecai and Esther, also known as Hadassah, who becomes queen (Esther 2:5–17). We'll cover all three in upcoming chapters.

If we're the youngest or ever consider ourselves to be the least, are we willing to let God's perspective inform our self-image? What role does God want us to play in our family?

[Read about Benjamin throughout Genesis 42–45. Discover more in Genesis 35:18 and Genesis 49:27.]

56. ER (1)

Jacob's son Judah leaves his family and travels to Adullam. There he marries a Canaanite woman, a descendant of Canaan, which as a group Noah cursed.

They have three sons. The oldest is Er, followed by Onan, and then Shelah.

Judah finds a wife for his firstborn son, Er. Her name is Tamar (1).

All we know about Er is that he is wicked in God's sight, so God kills him.

Does this idea of being wicked in God's sight sound familiar? Back in the days of Noah, God saw the wickedness of all people and destroyed them with a flood.

Though we don't know the details about Er's wicked behavior, we do know it was severe enough for God to end his life right away. Though we all deserve death for our sins, it's seldom immediate. Er's punishment, however, is swift and final.

Thankfully, Jesus will later provide a solution to the death sentence we all face.

How does knowing that God sees all our sins affect us? Though none of us are as wicked as Er, our sins do separate us from God. Have you turned to Jesus to be reconciled with the Father?

[Read about Er in Genesis 38:6–7. Discover more about wickedness in Genesis 6:5–6.]

57. ONAN

After God kills Er for his extreme wickedness, Er's father, Judah, passes the dead man's widow, Tamar (1), to his second child, Onan. The intent is that Onan will produce children for his deceased brother to carry on his family line through Tamar.

Judah tells Onan it's his responsibility as Tamar's brother-in-law to do this.

Onan complies only in part. Though Onan uses Tamar to satisfy himself, he keeps her from getting pregnant. In doing so, he fails to obey his father and do what's expected of him.

God is not pleased. He views Onan's act as wicked.

Some take this story as confirmation that birth control displeases God, but the context focuses on Onan's failure to produce a child for his sister-in-law.

Though this expectation is distasteful to us today, it was the custom back then. And Onan fails to fulfill his responsibility.

God views it as wicked and kills Onan right away, just like he did with Onan's brother Er.

When have we not done what our parents told us to do? How does God view our disobedience?

[Read about Onan in Genesis 38:8–10. Discover more in a parallel story in Matthew 22:23–28.]

58. SHELAH (3)

God has killed Shelah's older brothers, Er and Onan, for their extreme wickedness.

The custom of the people is that Er's widow, Tamar (1), should be passed to the third brother so he can produce offspring through her for his dead brother. But Shelah isn't old enough. So Judah sends Tamar home to live with her parents until Shelah grows up, pledging that she will one day marry him.

Yet Judah doesn't follow through on his promise to Tamar. He fears that Shelah will die just like Er and Onan. This suggests that Judah may blame Tamar for his sons' deaths. He doesn't want to risk the life of his only remaining son, so he withholds Shelah from Tamar.

As a result, Tamar takes extreme action to get what is due to her and what Judah promised to give.

Though Shelah's presence brings about these events, he does nothing good or bad to make them happen.

We know nothing about his character. But we do know that God views his older brothers as wicked and doesn't proclaim the same judgment on Shelah.

This suggests that Shelah isn't like his brothers and chooses a better path.

What negative traits of our family and friends should we avoid? What admirable traits of our family and friends should we follow?

[Read about Shelah in Genesis 38:11–14. Discover another son who stood out from his brothers in 1 Samuel 16:1–13.]

59. PEREZ

fter Tamar (1) tricks Judah into impregnating her, she gives birth to twins. They are Perez and Zerah.

The name Perez means "breaking out," because he broke out of the womb first before his twin brother.

Though we know nothing more about Perez and what he did, future generations esteem him. When Boaz marries the widowed and childless Ruth several centuries later, the townspeople proclaim blessings on her. They say, "may your family be like that of Perez, whom Tamar bore to Judah" (Ruth 4:12).

And this blessing comes to be.

Ruth has Obed, who is the father of Jesse and the grandfather of King David. Matthew's genealogy of Jesus honors all four (Matthew 1:5–6), as with their ancestor Perez (Matthew 1:3).

Though Perez's conception occurred in a duplicitous situation, he made his life matter.

What can we do to make our lives matter? How can we rise above our circumstances and not let them define us?

[Read about Perez in Genesis 38:27–30. Discover more in Luke 3:33.]

60. ZERAH (3)

Zerah is the younger twin of Perez. They are sons of Judah and Tamar (1).

When Tamar is in labor, the hand of one of her babies emerges. The midwife ties a scarlet thread around his wrist. Then the hand withdraws.

The baby who is born first, however, doesn't have the scarlet thread around his wrist. The baby who's born second, does. They name him Zerah, which means "scarlet" or "brightness."

Though Zerah is nearly born first, he isn't. His brother Perez beats him. Birth order is important to the people at that time. As a result, Zerah's parents elevate Perez's life over Zerah's.

Zerah no doubt grew up hearing the story of his hand emerging first and the midwife tying a scarlet thread around it. But his brother enters the world before him.

We can suspect Zerah spends his life wondering what might have happened had he been born first.

In what areas of our lives do we wonder what might have been? How can we move beyond what we wish had happened in the past to make a difference today?

[Read about Zerah in Genesis 38:27–30. Discover another set of twins in Genesis 25:21–34.]

61. POTIPHAR'S WIFE

Joseph is an attractive man. Potiphar's wife notices. She pursues Joseph.

We don't know her motivation. Does her husband ignore her? Is she bored? Perhaps she's merely promiscuous. Yet her reasons don't matter. She tries to seduce Joseph.

Joseph resists. He explains why he won't sleep with her, but she ignores his words, focusing only on her lust to be with him. This goes on day after day.

Joseph strives to stay away from her or makes sure someone is always around whenever she's nearby. But one day, as he goes about his work, she realizes they are alone. She becomes aggressive. She grabs him and draws him toward her. He pulls away. In his haste to escape her grasp, he leaves his cloak in her hands as he flees.

Unable to satisfy her desires, her lust turns to revenge.

She calls for her servants and spins a lie about what happened, of how Joseph pursued her, of how she screamed for help, and of how he ran off. She holds up his jacket as proof. When Potiphar gets home, she repeats her lies to him. In a rage, he throws Joseph in prison, where he languishes for years.

Potiphar's wife is an immoral woman who makes no effort to

control her sexual desires. She is an unfaithful spouse—or at least she tries to be one. When she can't seduce Joseph or convince him to sleep with her, she concocts lies to destroy him.

How far will we go to get what we want, even when it's wrong? How low will we stoop to hurt those who get in our way?

[Read about Potiphar's wife in Genesis 39:1–20. Discover a different encounter in 2 Samuel 13:1–19.]

62. POTIPHAR

Through a series of events outside his control, Joseph has become a slave owned by Potiphar. Potiphar is one of Pharaoh's officials and captain of the guard.

God's favor is on Joseph in Potiphar's household, and he proves himself to the captain. Potiphar eventually puts his entire estate under the care of his slave. Potiphar's home and property prosper because of Joseph's diligent work and God's blessing on him.

Joseph conducts himself so well that Potiphar trusts him with everything. His only concern at home is what he will eat. Joseph handles all else.

But one day this perfect situation falls apart. Potiphar's wife comes to him in a rage, claiming that Joseph tried to rape her.

Furious, Potiphar throws Joseph into prison.

Though we may assume Potiphar does this because of what he believes Joseph did, why didn't he take a harsher action? As captain of the guard, we can assume he has the power to do something more punitive than prison. And since Joseph is a slave, he has no rights. Could Potiphar have used his power to execute Joseph?

But what if prison is an act of mercy, something done out of esteem for Joseph? Perhaps Potiphar suspects his wife is to blame and not his servant. Has she cheated on him in the past? What if Potiphar knows in his spirit that Joseph is innocent, that he's the victim?

If this is the case, Potiphar can't punish his wife without the situation becoming public. And if he dismisses her allegations by doing nothing, that would only strain his relationship with his wife even more. In this instance, we see that throwing Joseph in prison is the easiest recourse for Potiphar.

Regardless of the reasons behind Potiphar's actions, the fact remains that innocent Joseph lands in prison.

When we hear a condemning story about someone, do we believe it or try to verify the truth? How can we rectify our mistake when we believe what someone told us, only to later learn it was a lie?

[Read about Potiphar in Genesis 39:1–20. Discover what happens to Joseph next in Genesis 40.]

63. ASENATH

Pharaoh later gives the-now-freed Joseph a wife. Her name is Asenath, and she's the daughter of the priest of On. The priest's name is Potiphera. (Don't confuse Potiphera with Potiphar.) This is likely a strategic move on Pharaoh's part, hoping that Asenath will influence Joseph to accept Egyptian perspectives and beliefs.

In this way, Pharaoh uses Asenath to accomplish his goal. He expects her to influence her husband for her country. But she has no say in his plan.

We know Joseph is both attractive and powerful, but he's also an outsider. He isn't even permitted to eat at the same table as the Egyptians. Asenath is forced to marry a foreigner. There is no hint of love or affection between the two. Though this could be a good life for her, it's doubtful it's the one she wanted.

Asenath and Joseph have two sons, Manasseh and Ephraim, but we know nothing else of the couple's relationship. We don't know if Joseph influences his wife to believe in God, but in looking at the life of Joseph, we see no hint that Asenath causes him to embrace her people's way of life or turn from God.

*When others try to use us, do we become their pawn or make our own path?
How should we react if we're in a marriage we don't want?*

[Read about Asenath in Genesis 41:45–50. Discover a man whose foreign wives influenced him in 1 Kings 11:1–13.]

64. MANASSEH AND EPHRAIM

Joseph and Asenath have two sons. The oldest is Manasseh, and the younger is Ephraim. They are the grandsons of Jacob, later called Israel.

When Israel is on his deathbed, Joseph comes to see his ailing father, bringing his two sons, Manasseh and Ephraim, with him. Hearing about Joseph's arrival, Israel rallies and sits up in bed.

He makes a curious statement to his son. Israel elevates his two grandsons, Manasseh and Ephraim, and mentions them along with his own sons. In this way, Israel grants these two boys the same status as their uncles. All will receive their inheritance through Israel. This, in effect, gives Joseph's descendants a double portion, something due to the firstborn son.

Though Joseph is not Israel's firstborn, he is Rachel's. Since the now-deceased Rachel was Israel's favorite wife, we can understand him seeking to give Joseph a double portion through his boys.

Israel first blesses Joseph. Next, he blesses Manasseh and Ephraim. Israel, however, blesses Ephraim as the older son and Manasseh as the younger.

When Joseph tries to correct his father's error, Israel confirms it is not a mistake. He declares that the younger Ephraim will be greater than the older Manasseh.

Yet we don't see much in Scripture to indicate that Ephraim does in fact become greater than Manasseh.

Four centuries later, when Israel's numerous descendants leave Egypt, Moses notes that Ephraim's tribe numbers 40,500, with Manasseh's tribe about 20 percent less at 32,200. Yet forty years later when they leave the desert, things are the opposite. Manasseh's descendants have increased to 52,700, while the number of Ephraim's descendants have shrunk to 32,500.

We should keep in mind that during these forty years in the desert, all who entered it died there (except for Joshua and Caleb). It is their offspring that the second census counts. Therefore, Manasseh's tribe flourished in the desert and Ephraim's did not.

When they reach the promised land, Manasseh's descendants divide into two groups, with half receiving an inheritance east of the Jordan and the rest, west of the Jordan. Each group becomes a half tribe of Manasseh.

If anything, it seems that Manasseh becomes greater than Ephraim, despite Israel's blessing.

Do we let our birth order define us? When someone proclaims a blessing over us, how much confidence do we place in their words?

[Read about Manasseh and Ephraim in Genesis 48:1–20. Discover more in Numbers 1:32–35 and Numbers 26:34–37.]

65. SHIPHRAH AND PUAH (2)

S hiphrah and Puah are two Hebrew midwives. They live toward the end of the Israelites' enslavement in Egypt.

The Pharaoh of Egypt, fearing their slaves' mounting numbers, tells Shiphrah and Puah to kill all the baby Israelite boys as they are being born. This is worse than, in effect, performing abortions. It is euthanasia.

But Shiphrah and Puah fear God more than Egypt's pharaoh. So they disregard the king's order and continue to attend to the birth of the Israelite boys, doing everything they can to ensure their survival.

When the Pharaoh confronts them for not doing as he commanded, the two midwives lie. They tell him they don't arrive in time to do anything. Pharaoh accepts their excuse.

Though they did lie to the Pharaoh, God honors them for their integrity in protecting the Israelite baby boys. He rewards them, giving them their own families.

Sometimes doing the right thing means disobeying human authority and manmade laws. God may honor us as a result, but we could also suffer consequences for our actions.

We should strive to do what God wants us to, regardless of the risk or the outcome.

How willing are we to do what is right? Is lying to protect ourselves ever a justifiable action?

[Read about Shiphrah and Puah in Exodus 1:15–21. Discover more about another woman who lied in Genesis 31:33–35.]

MOSES AND THE LAW

Jacob and his family end up in Egypt because of a famine. When the famine ends, they don't go home to the land God promised Abraham, but they stay in Egypt. There their numbers explode, and the Egyptians force them into slavery.

Four centuries later, Moses arrives and eventually leads them to freedom and back to the promised land. He also receives God's instructions for right living, which we refer to as the Law, the Law of Moses. This tells the people what to do and not to do so that they may be right with God.

After Moses, we'll continue our biblical story arc to Joshua, the judges, and the people begging for a king to lead them instead of God. But first we must cover someone else, someone you may have never heard about.

66. JOCHEBED

After the seven-year famine ends, Jacob and his family don't go home. Instead, they stay in Egypt. They prosper there and remain for four centuries. This is where we pick up our story.

In the intervening years, the Egyptians have enslaved Jacob's offspring, forcing them to do manual labor for their building projects. Fearing the mushrooming population of the Israelites, Pharaoh orders his people to throw every Hebrew baby boy into the Nile River.

One mother, however, senses something unique in her child and decides to ignore the edict. She hides her son for as long as she can. Eventually, unable to conceal him any longer, she does put him in the Nile River, but not before laying him in a watertight basket.

She strategically places the basket where a compassionate person might find it. The woman's daughter hides nearby to see what happens to her baby brother.

When Pharaoh's daughter comes to the river to bathe, she discovers the baby and wants to keep him as her own. The baby's sister steps out of hiding and offers to find a woman to nurse him; she gets her mother. Although the boy should die, Pharaoh's daughter saves him and even pays his biological mother to care for him.

Once weaned, his mother gives him back to Pharaoh's daughter, who names him Moses. This Hebrew mother's name is Jochebed and she has two other children, Aaron and Miriam.

Jochebed, like many moms, sees promise in her child and takes extraordinary measures to protect him so he can reach his potential.

Who has seen promise in us and made a difference in our lives? Who can we help reach their potential?

[Read about Jochebed in Exodus 2:1–10. Discover more in Numbers 26:59.]

67. MOSES

Moses receives more coverage in the Old Testament than any other character, except for King David. Abraham comes in third.

Though we could compose an entire book about Moses—and others have—let's consider five defining moments in his life. We can use these to inspire and challenge us.

For our first story, let's look at Moses being raised in the palace. He senses his calling from the Lord to lead the people and goes out to visit them. There he encounters an Egyptian mistreating one of God's people. Moses kills the Egyptian and hides the body. When he learns his homicidal act is known, he takes off to build a new life away from Egypt and his people.

Next, Moses marries and cares for his father-in-law's flocks. While out in the wilderness doing his job, Moses spots a bush ablaze in the distance that does not burn up. He investigates. There he encounters God, who sends Moses back to Egypt to rescue his people. After debating a bit with the Almighty, Moses obeys.

Third, after a series of plagues sent by God and corresponding confrontations with Pharaoh, Moses leads the people out of Egypt. In one of the Bible's best-known stories, God parts the waters of the

Red Sea, and Moses leads his people to safety on the other side. When the Egyptian army gives chase, the waters crash down upon them, and they drown. Though God orchestrates this miracle, it occurs through Moses and is a result of his faith and obedience.

Another well-known story occurs when Moses is on a mountain communing with God where he receives instructions—the Ten Commandments and the Law. This at last gives the people God's rules for right living and proper conduct.

Though they may have had some inborn idea of right and wrong all along, now they understand for sure what God expects of them. They know that murder is wrong. They know that marrying a half-sister is wrong. And they know that worshiping anything other than God is wrong.

It takes time for God to give Moses his rules, and the people grow impatient. Aaron acts. He fashions an idol made from gold—a golden calf—and institutes a raucous worship celebration of the statue.

God is furious at the people and wants to wipe them out. He promises to start over and make a new nation, not of Abraham's seed, but from Moses's. Instead of accepting God's plan to make him into a great nation, Moses intercedes for the rebellious people. God hears his plea and relents. The people live because of Moses.

Last, aside from committing homicide much earlier in his life, Moses later mars his otherwise exemplary leadership by a single act of disobedience. The people are thirsty and clamor for water. God tells Moses to go to a rock and speak to it. Then water will flow forth.

Though Moses does go to the rock, he hits it twice with his staff. And instead of speaking the words God gave him, Moses utters his own. By doing so, he dishonors the Lord. Because of this single sin God won't let Moses enter the promised land.

This is a poignant reminder that if we try to approach God by following a bunch of rules—such as the Law he gave to Moses and the people—even one failure, in one area, is sufficient to disqualify us from our heavenly reward.

Fortunately, Jesus came to show us another way, something

anyone can do. It's simple. All we need to do is put our faith in him (Ephesians 2:8–9).

What examples from Moses's life should we aspire to? How can we have a close, intimate relationship with God just like Moses?

[Read about Moses throughout Exodus, Leviticus, Numbers, and Deuteronomy. Discover more in John 3:14, Acts 7:20–44, 2 Corinthians 3:7–13, and Hebrews 11:23–29.]

68. AARON

Aaron is the older brother of Moses. His mother is Jochebed, and his father is Amram.

God tells Aaron to go out into the wilderness to meet Moses, who is expecting him. The plan is for Aaron to serve as his brother's spokesman, because Moses doesn't think he's eloquent enough for the job God called him to do.

Aaron and Moses work together to communicate with Pharaoh and bring about the people's eventual escape from Egypt. When God gives Moses the Law, Aaron and his sons will play a vital role in leading the people in worship. In doing so, Aaron becomes the first priest, and his sons—at least the two obedient ones—continue the work, as will their descendants.

Aaron does all God asks of him, supports his younger brother Moses, and serves well as God's first priest. Despite all this exemplary behavior, however, Aaron has two blemishes in his otherwise spotless record.

Before God institutes Aaron as his priest, Aaron attempts to assume this responsibility himself. As we already learned in the chapter about Moses, it's Aaron who constructs the golden calf idol and leads the people to worship it. This isn't what God intended.

The other incident occurs later.

Aaron and Miriam criticize Moses for his choice of a wife. They also attempt to elevate themselves as spokespeople for God, since the Almighty also talks to them and not just Moses.

God hears their murmuring and isn't pleased. He burns with anger toward them for opposing Moses and seeking to promote themselves.

The Almighty strikes Miriam with leprosy, and Aaron panics. He begs Moses for forgiveness. The fact he doesn't go directly to God suggests he doesn't have as close of a relationship with the Almighty as he and Miriam thought.

Aaron escapes punishment, perhaps because he so quickly sought forgiveness.

When we sin are we quick to confess it and seek forgiveness? Have we ever attempted to elevate ourselves beyond what God has called us to do?

[Read about Aaron in Exodus 4–12 and Exodus 16–19. Discover more in Deuteronomy 10:6 and Luke 1:5.]

69. MIRIAM (1)

Miriam is the older sister of Moses and the sister of Aaron. Recall that young Miriam watches at a distance to see what happens after her mom places baby Moses in a basket in the Nile River. In this we see an obedient and brave girl.

Later, as an adult, Miriam becomes both a prophet and a worship leader. She directs the Israelite women in song and dance to celebrate God's rescue after they cross the sea to escape the pursuing Egyptian army.

Unfortunately, what we know best about Miriam is when she and Aaron oppose Moses out of jealousy, criticizing his choice for a wife. God's judgment is quick, instantly afflicting her with leprosy, a contagious skin disease, which was untreatable at the time.

Though Aaron is also at fault, he doesn't get leprosy. This suggests that Miriam led their tiny rebellion. Aaron sees what happened and admits his bad attitude, begging Moses to intervene. Moses does, and God implicitly heals Miriam.

A few years later Miriam dies. There's no mention of the people mourning her death. This is a sad end to a once-promising life. Though Miriam starts well as a brave and obedient daughter and later becomes a prophet and worship leader, she lets jealousy define her later life. God is not pleased.

What can we do to finish strong? When we falter, how do we react when confronted with our shortcomings?

[Read about Miriam in Exodus 2:1–10, Exodus 15:20–21, Numbers 12:1–15, and Numbers 20:1. Discover another person whose behavior resulted in leprosy in 2 Kings 5.]

70. REUEL (2)/JETHRO

When Moses flees Egypt for his life, he ends up in the desert. There he encounters the seven daughters of Reuel, a Midianite priest. The girls are shepherdesses. When they try to draw water from the well for their sheep, however, other shepherds drive them away. Moses intervenes for them and waters their flock.

Reuel (later called Jethro) is grateful, and he invites Moses to stay with them. He gives his daughter Zipporah to Moses in marriage.

The next time we encounter Reuel in the Bible is several years later. This is after Moses leads his people out of Egypt. The Bible now calls him Jethro. We don't know why Reuel changed his name, but he did.

Jethro goes to the desert to meet Moses, returning Moses's wife and sons to him. Moses tells Jethro all that God has done, and Jethro praises the Almighty.

The next day he watches as Moses takes a seat to judge the people as they gather to receive his ruling on their cases. This takes all day. Jethro realizes this is too much for Moses to handle on his own. He advises his son-in-law to train capable men to hear the easier cases. Only the most complicated ones will need Moses's attention. This will lighten Moses's load of leading the people.

Moses follows his father-in-law's wise advice.

How open are we to follow the recommendations of others? Should we give advice to people who haven't asked for it?

[Read about Reuel in Exodus 2:16–21. Read about Jethro in Exodus 18. Discover more in Exodus 4:18.]

71. ZIPPORAH

When Moses flees for his life, he meets seven shepherdesses, the daughters of Reuel. Moses marries one of the daughters, Zipporah. Moses and Zipporah have two sons. They are Gershom and Eliezer.

Years later when Moses and his family travel to Egypt, God afflicts Moses. This is apparently because Moses failed to circumcise his son Gershom, as God commanded the Israelites to do through Abraham.

Just as God is about to kill Moses for his disobedience, Zipporah acts. She pulls out a knife and circumcises Gershom. She touches Moses with the removed foreskin. This appeases God, and he spares Moses.

Zipporah does what her husband did not do. She obeys God's command and saves her husband's life.

How willing are we to act when others fail to? How can we discern when to intervene and when not to?

[Read about Zipporah in Exodus 2:21–22 and Exodus 4:24–26. Discover more in Exodus 18:2–6.]

72. CALEB (1)

After the Hebrew people escape Egypt, they make their way across the desert, approaching the land God promised to Abraham. Moses selects a representative from each tribe of Israel to spy out the land.

Caleb, son of Jephunneh, is one of the twelve men selected, representing the tribe of Judah. The twelve head out to discover what the land is like and do some reconnaissance so they can form a battle plan to conquer it. They spend forty days making a comprehensive tour of the area.

The group returns and presents their findings to Moses. "It's a wonderful land," they say, "but the people who live there are powerful and reside in fortified cities."

Caleb, however, offers an opposite perspective. His is the minority report. "We should leave at once and conquer the land. We can certainly do that."

But the majority disagree with Caleb. The Israelites—whose only skill is slave labor—seem no match for the inhabitants of the land. "Those people are stronger and bigger than we are," they say.

In the end, the people disregard what Caleb said and believe the majority report. They cry, grumble, and want to return to Egypt.

But Caleb—along with Joshua, one of the other spies—encourages the people to move forward under God's power to take the land.

In response, the people threaten to stone them.

Are we willing to stand up and speak God's truth even if we are a small minority? When we see others deciding to do what we believe is wrong, how do we respond?

[Read about Caleb in Numbers 13–14. Discover more in Joshua 15:13–19 and Judges 1:12–20.]

73. JOSHUA (1)

Joshua son of Nun serves Moses, first as an aide and later as his protégé, before he eventually succeeds him. Joshua is first known as Hoshea, but Moses gives him the name of Joshua. Though there's much to examine in Joshua's life, let's focus on a few significant moments.

The young apprentice witnesses his mentor's example and is often present when Moses interacts with God. What an amazing experience this must have been. It shouldn't surprise us that Moses selects Joshua as one of the twelve men chosen to spy out the land in preparation for conquering it.

What seems strange is Joshua's silence when Caleb gives his recommendation to go at once to take the land. Caleb seems to stand alone against the other spies who cower in fear.

Joshua, however, later joins Caleb to counter the majority report as the pair try to convince the people to move forward in faith, under God's power. They continue their efforts, until the people threaten to kill them.

About forty years later, when Moses dies, Joshua succeeds him. He successfully leads the people to conquer the promised land. Though an entire generation has died in the desert because of their grumbling and lack of faith, Joshua and Caleb are still alive. Joshua rewards Caleb's faithfulness by assigning him a portion of the land the people conquered.

Joshua dies at 110 years old. Although Moses wisely appointed Joshua as his successor, Joshua fails to follow his mentor's example. He dies without having groomed anyone to replace him.

When we fail to speak up when we should, what can we do to correct our error? What are we doing to ensure that what we have started can continue when we're gone?

[Read about Joshua in Exodus 17:9–14 and Numbers 13–14, as well as the entire book of Joshua. Discover more in Numbers 18–23, Deuteronomy 3:21–28, and Deuteronomy 31.]

74. GERSHOM (1) AND ELIEZER (2)

Moses and Zipporah have two sons, Gershom and Eliezer.

The oldest is Gershom. His name means *a foreigner there* because Moses says he's a foreigner in a foreign land.

The younger son is Eliezer. His name means *God is my helper*. Moses acknowledges God as the helper who saved him from Pharaoh's attempt to kill him.

When we consider Moses's close relationship with God and how he successfully leads God's people from Egypt to the promised land, we expect to see this carry over to Moses's boys. Yet the Bible doesn't say this happens.

Instead, Gershom and Eliezer lead unremarkable lives. Scripture doesn't show them as walking closely with the Almighty like their father. Nor does it portray them in any sort of leadership capacity.

Moses could have modeled his deep relationship with God for Gershom and Eliezer to emulate. But there's no indication he did, contrary to the command God gave the people through Moses (Deuteronomy 6:6–9).

Moses could have trained his boys to follow him in leadership, but he did not. It's Moses's protégé, Joshua, who takes over for the exceptional leader and not Moses's sons.

Gershom and Eliezer accomplish nothing noteworthy.

What must we do to pass our faith on to our family and those under our influence? If we come from a strong legacy, what are we doing to continue it?

[Read about Gershom and Eliezer in Exodus 18:2–4. Discover more in 1 Chronicles 23:15–17.]

75. JANNES AND JAMBRES

It may surprise you to see Jannes and Jambres in our discussion of Old Testament sinners and saints. This is because they don't appear in the Old Testament. They show up in the New Testament and then only once. Yet the reference ties them to Moses, so this places them in the Old Testament timeline.

Paul, in writing to his protégé Timothy, talks about how people will act in the last days. (It's a description that seems most apt to our world today.)

Paul warns Timothy to have nothing to do with such people. The teacher goes on to explain why. These people oppose truth, just as Jannes and Jambres opposed Moses.

We can surmise that the story of Jannes and Jambres is part of the Hebrew oral tradition passed down from one generation to the next, which Timothy would have heard from his grandmother Lois and mother Eunice. But we're left to speculate what this opposition might have been. With Moses facing much resistance as the leader of God's chosen people, we have many scenarios to choose from.

Though we don't know the specifics, we can be sure that Timothy does. Paul equates the opposition that Timothy will face with the opposition that Moses faced.

We are safe to assume that Moses prevailed against his foes. In this way, Timothy receives encouragement to prevail in his situation against those who will oppose him. Surely this heartens the young leader.

Who can we encourage on their faith journey? What from our family's oral tradition should we teach to encourage future generations?

[Read about Jannes and Jambres in 2 Timothy 3:8. Discover more about opposition in Exodus 23:20–22.]

76. BALAK

Because of the people's lack of faith, God turns them away from the promised land. They spend forty years in the desert, one year for each day the spies were on their mission. We resume our story four decades later as they finally prepare to conquer the nations before them under the leadership of Moses and then Joshua.

Balak son of Zippor, king of Moab, sees the approaching Hebrew people and fears they will attack his land. Believing he cannot prevail with military force alone, he sends for Balaam, a practitioner of divination, to curse the encroaching horde.

Balaam refuses, but Balak persists. When Balaam agrees to appear before Balak, he repeatedly reminds the king and his emissaries that he can only say what the Lord puts in his mouth.

Balak accepts this condition. He sacrifices seven bulls and seven rams as Balaam instructs. Then, prompted by God, Balaam blesses the Hebrew people.

Frustrated that Balaam didn't dispense curses as requested, the desperate Balak asks Balaam to try again. The outcome is the same.

Having not learned his lesson, Balak begs Balaam a third time to spew forth curses against the danger that threatens Moab. Once again, Balaam speaks blessings instead of curses.

Balak is furious with Balaam. Yet it's his own fault. Balaam declined to come to Balak in the first place and warned he could only say what God told him to say.

But Balak was too afraid and pushed forward when he shouldn't have. His ill-advised actions in seeking to curse his enemies had the opposite effect.

When has our fear caused us to do the wrong thing? When have we failed to see God at work and persisted to pursue our own path?

[Read about Balak in Numbers 22–24. Discover more in Micah 6:5 and Revelation 2:14.]

77. BALAAM

Balaam son of Beor practices divination. His work must be of some renown, for when Balak seeks a supernatural edge over the approaching Hebrew people, he sends for Balaam to proclaim curses against the Israelites.

God tells Balaam not to go and he doesn't. We affirm him for doing what God said.

But Balak persists and sends a second delegation to fetch Balaam. The seer again seeks a word from God about what to do, even though the Almighty had already made his position clear. This time God says to go but for Balaam to watch what he says, speaking only the words God gives him to say.

At each step of the story Balaam does exactly what God tells him to do. We can applaud him for his obedience.

Yet not so fast.

In the end, God isn't pleased with Balaam. We're left to wonder why, for it seems Balaam obeyed God flawlessly and did everything as instructed.

But the hint for God's displeasure comes from what Balaam did after the second emissary delegation arrived. Though God had already made it clear Balaam wasn't to go, the greedy seer asked a second time. Instead of repeating his prior instruction, God relented and allowed Balaam to go.

Though this is what the prophet desired to do all along, it wasn't what God wanted. The rest of Scripture confirms God's displeasure with Balaam.

When we don't like what God tells us to do, do we keep asking anyway? Might there have ever been a time when we thought we were being obedient, yet our attitude displeased God?

[Read about Balaam in Numbers 22–24. Discover more in Numbers 31:8, 2 Peter 2:15–16, Jude 1:11, and Revelation 2:14.]

78. NADAB (1) AND ABIHU

Aaron has four sons. They are Nadab, Abihu, Eleazar, and Ithamar. With Aaron as the first priest, all four boys are destined to follow him. With Nadab and Abihu as the oldest two, they take the lead in this.

Nadab and Abihu, however, fail to follow God's precise guidelines of worship. Whether it's sloppiness or arrogance, we don't know, but they offer fire and incense to God, contrary to his command. Scripture calls it "unauthorized fire."

As a result of their disobedience, God sends fire to kill them. God's punishment is swift and final.

The Almighty doesn't offer them mercy for their disobedience, just judgment. But fortunately for us today, through Jesus, we can receive the Lord's mercy.

What would we change in our lives if God punished us immediately? When have we relied on God's mercy and grace when we should have stopped doing something wrong?

[Read about Nadab and Abihu in Leviticus 10:1–3, as well as Numbers 26:60–61. Discover more in Numbers 3:1–4.]

79. ELEAZAR (1) AND ITHAMAR

God strikes down Nadab and Abihu for their disobedience. Without any heirs, this means that all the priestly duties now fall to their brothers, Eleazar and Ithamar.

Though all four brothers should have served God together, the work now goes to the two remaining sons of Aaron. As a result, they have twice as much work to do.

As they serve God, we can suspect they do so with much care, remembering the immediate deaths of their brothers for not diligently following God's detailed instructions. They've seen firsthand what could happen if they disobey. This surely guides them and their work for the rest of their lives.

Though we see nothing in Scripture to confirm the work they do, we also don't see anything to criticize it. We can, therefore, assume that God affirms their work as his priests.

There is one incident, however, where things could have gone awry. Right after their older brothers die, Uncle Moses gives Eleazar and Ithamar some instructions on making offerings. They don't do everything Moses expected, and he's angry. Their father, Aaron, however, intervenes on their behalf, and Moses takes no action against them.

God's silence in this matter suggests he's not concerned about what these two priests did.

When have we criticized someone when God may not have cared? How can we discern between knowing when to stand up for God and when to be silent?

[Read about Eleazar and Ithamar in Leviticus 10:6–20. Discover more in Numbers 3:4.]

80. KORAH (3)

Korah is the son of Izhar, the son of Kohath, the son of Levi. He leads a rebellion against Aaron, Moses . . . and God.

The descendants of Levi are set apart from the rest of the Israelites for a special role. They are to work in the tabernacle and assist the priests in ministering to the people. But this isn't enough for Korah. He wants to be a priest too.

He brings with him three men from the tribe of Reuben. They are Dathan, Abiram, and On. And they rally 250 men to join them. They all want to serve as priests and don't feel this role is only for descendants of Aaron.

Though they may be doing this to elevate themselves into a more prominent position, they could also have pure motives, wanting to serve God more fully. Yet this doesn't make it right.

Korah challenges Moses. Distraught, Moses proposes a spiritual showdown.

The next day, Korah and his followers are to each take a censer with fire and incense to present to the Lord. Aaron will do the same. Then God will pick who he wants.

The actions and attitudes of Korah and his followers displease

God. He reacts immediately. The ground opens and swallows Korah, Dathan, and Abiram, their families, and their possessions. Then God sends fire from heaven to consume the 250 men offering incense.

God makes it clear he wants only Aaron (and later his descendants) to serve him as priest.

When have our spiritual aspirations not pleased God? How can we discern when to strive for more and when to be content with the position God has given us?

[Read about Korah in Numbers 16. Discover more in Exodus 6:18–24.]

81. PHINEHAS (1)

Phinehas is the son of Eleazar, the son of Aaron. This means that Phinehas is Aaron's grandson.

While the Israelites are in the desert getting ready to take the promised land, an issue of sexual immorality arises between some of the men and Moabite women. This effectively aligns them with Baal. The Lord is infuriated and orders their execution.

Even as the people mourn the death of these men, one Israelite man doesn't understand—or doesn't care. He brings a Midianite woman into camp and into his tent. Everyone sees this. It's as if he's flaunting what he's going to do.

Phinehas won't have it. He grabs a spear. Going into the man's tent, he drives it through the man and into the woman. God's anger subsides. A plague that has already killed 24,000 people stops.

Though we may question Phinehas for his judgment and violent action, God does not. He implicitly affirms it.

But it's an overstretch to interpret this passage as advocating violence—even murder—in God's name. A better conclusion is to be ready to take decisive action for the things that matter to God.

Phinehas acted with zeal, and this pleased God.

In what is a likely connection, Phinehas emerges as the leading priest among his generation.

When have we been passive when we should have acted? When have we overreacted when a more God-honoring approach would have been moderation?

[Read about Phinehas in Numbers 25:6–13. Discover more in Numbers 31:6–7 and Joshua 22:13–33.]

82. KOZBI

The nation of Israel has a problem with sexual immorality. Some of their men are involved with Moabite women, indulging themselves sexually with these foreigners, something the law of Moses prohibits. Then these women entice the men to worship with them and offer sacrifices to Baal instead of God.

God is not pleased. Moses orders the execution of each man who has strayed.

During all this, another man brings a Midianite woman into camp and into his tent. Her name is Kozbi. We don't know if he thinks this is okay because she is a Midianite and not a Moabite. Perhaps he wants to make a point or maybe he isn't thinking at all. We also don't know if Kozbi is aware of the situation. What we do know is that this man flaunts his sexual relationship with a foreign woman, a liaison God forbids and for which many other men have just died.

Phinehas, the priest, takes judgment into his hands in the form of a spear. Going into the tent, he drives the shaft all the way through the man and into Kozbi. This appeases God's wrath.

While Kozbi may have instigated this, it's more likely she is merely a naïve woman who ends up in the wrong place. But she pays for her ignorance with her life.

Being unaware is no excuse for doing wrong. There will still be consequences for our actions.

What must we do to guard ourselves from sexual immorality? If we intentionally sin, do we rely on God's mercy or fear his judgment?

[Read about Kozbi in Numbers 25:6–18. Discover more in Numbers 25:1–5.]

83. ZELOPHEHAD

Zelophehad has five daughters but no sons. His girls are Mahlah, Noah (2), Hoglah, Milkah (2), and Tirzah. Zelophehad dies in the desert before he can receive his allotment of property in the promised land. Since he has no sons to receive his inheritance in his stead, the girls will get nothing.

They boldly go before Moses and ask for their father's share, contrary to convention. God tells Moses to include them in the land assignments, which Joshua later carries out.

With a population of millions, there are surely other women in this same situation. But only Zelophehad's daughters come forward.

In this way, Zelophehad's descendants receive property in the promised land.

Are we willing to speak up to receive what is due us? Will we trust God with the outcome?

[Read about Zelophehad in Numbers 27:1–7. Discover more in Numbers 36:1–12 and Joshua 17:3–6.]

84. ACHAN

At last it's time for Joshua to lead the people into the land God promised to give them and take it. First up is Jericho. But they don't attack the city as we'd expect. Instead, they march around it for seven days.

On the seventh day, the priests blow their trumpets, the people shout, and the walls fall. They burn the entire city and everything in it but keep the gold and silver, putting it into the treasury, just as God commanded. Only Rahab and her family survive (Joshua 6:17–25).

Next up is Ai. It's a small town with few inhabitants. The spies recommend that an army of two or three thousand can easily take the city. But Ai routs them and kills three dozen men.

Distraught, Joshua seeks God. That's when God shares that someone failed to follow his exacting instructions when taking Jericho.

When God reveals that the guilty person is Achan, he admits his sin in taking a beautiful robe, silver, and gold from the city and hiding them in his tent.

Though he confesses his sin, he doesn't receive forgiveness.

Instead, he receives judgment. The people stone him to death, along with his family and possessions. Then they burn everything.

With God's wrath now appeased, the people attack the city of Ai. This time they do exactly what God says. This time they're victorious (Joshua 8:1–29).

How well do we do at obeying God's commands? When have we last thanked Jesus for forgiving our sins?

[Read about Achan in Joshua 7. Discover another person who failed to obey God's command to utterly destroy a city in 1 Samuel 15:1–31.]

85. RAHAB

The Hebrew people's first opportunity to take the promised land didn't work out. Forty years after this first failure, Joshua—who is now in charge—sends out two spies instead of twelve.

As the two spies explore Jericho, they stay with Rahab, a prostitute. We don't know if they seek her for her services or merely for a place to hide from public view.

Learning of their presence, Jericho's king commands Rahab to turn over the two men. In a treasonous act, she hides them instead. She lies to the king, saying they've already left, but that she doesn't know where they went.

Rahab realizes God favors Israel and that he will give the city to them. In exchange for protecting the spies, she asks for her family's safety. Joshua promises to spare Rahab and her family when the Israelites raze the city. After the destruction of Jericho and its inhabitants, Rahab goes to live with the Israelites.

In the New Testament, Matthew reveals Rahab as one of Jesus's direct ancestors and the great-great-grandmother of King David.

She's honored as only one of four women listed in Jesus's family tree. She's also affirmed as a person of faith, one of only two women included in the list of God's most faithful followers in Hebrews 11.

Finally, James confirms Rahab is righteous because of her courageous actions in protecting the two spies.

While our reaction may be to judge Rahab for her profession, God sees her differently, as a woman of faith. He rewards her accordingly. He doesn't judge her by her work, but he does affirm her for her faith.

When have we judged someone because of their job or reputation? How can we better appreciate the people God affirms?

[Read about Rahab in Joshua 2:1–21 and 6:17–25. Discover more in Matthew 1:1–5, Hebrews 11:31, and James 2:25.]

86. EHUD (1)

It takes some time for God's people to take possession of the land he promised them. Once they do, a distressing cycle recurs. They turn from God and do evil, he allows a foreign power to conquer them, and they cry out to the Lord for help. In response he sends them a judge—a military leader—to free them.

Such is the case with Ehud.

Because of the Israelites' disobedience to God, he allows the king of Moab to subject them to his control for eighteen years. When they cry out for help, he sends Ehud.

This story has two interesting elements. First, Ehud is left-handed. Second, the king of Moab is extremely overweight. Here's what happens.

Ehud leads the delegation to pay their annual tribute to Moab. After they complete their mission and leave, Ehud heads back. He tells the king he has a secret message to share.

The guards likely assumed Ehud is right-handed and looked for a weapon on his left as would be the norm, but not the other side. Therefore, Ehud's sword escapes detection.

The king sends everyone away. We can envision Ehud extending his right hand in a friendly gesture as he approaches the king to deliver the message. With the king distracted and feeling safe, Ehud stealthily draws his sword with his left hand and thrusts it into the King's belly. The 18-inch sword (close to half a meter) plunges into the king's belly and his fat covers the hilt.

Ehud locks the doors and flees through the terrace. He escapes before anyone realizes the king is dead.

Ehud summons the army, and they attack Moab, killing ten thousand of their troops. With this victory over their enemy, Moab is now subject to Israel. And the people live in peace for eighty years.

What bold action may God be calling us to make? Seeing how one person can make a difference, what can we do today?

[Read about Ehud in Judges 3:12–30. Discover a similar story in 2 Samuel 3:22–30.]

87. DEBORAH (2)

As we covered in the chapter on Joshua, he dies without naming a successor. A lack of leadership makes it hard for the people to keep their focus on God, and they languish as a nation. The book of Judges summarizes this succinctly: it is a time when Israel has no king, and everyone does whatever they want (Judges 21:25).

During this time, they encounter repeated cycles of disobedience, oppression, rescue, and obedience—only to fall back into ignoring God. The rescue portion of each cycle comes from a judge. This is not someone who decides legal cases. Instead, these judges are leaders, often military ones.

Though called a judge, Deborah is primarily a prophetess, a person who hears from God and proclaims his words to others. She is the only female judge in the book of Judges. And unlike the other judges listed, she's the only one to hold court.

Aligned with her primary calling, Deborah receives a prophetic message for Barak. Through her, God commands him to raise an army and attack their enemy. God even promises that Barak will prevail, but the fearful man declines.

Barak refuses to do what God tells him to do unless Deborah

goes with him. She consents but prophesies that because of his reluctance, the honor of killing the enemy's leader, Sisera, will go to a woman.

Deborah lives in a male-dominated society. Yet, when a man doesn't do what he's supposed to, she steps forward and acts. We commend her for her faith and her bravery.

When others won't do what they're supposed to do for God, are we willing to step in to help make it happen? Are we sometimes like Barak, lacking the courage to do what God tells us to do?

[Read about Deborah in Judges 4–5. Discover other prophetesses in Exodus 15:20, 2 Kings 22:14, and Luke 2:36-38.]

88. BARAK

God gives the prophetess Deborah a message for Barak. God wants him to raise a troop of 10,000 and confront the better-equipped army led by Sisera. God promises to give Barak the victory. But Barak balks.

Barak is the son of Abinoam. He lives in Kedesh in the territory of Naphtali in Israel. That's all we know about him. Though he might be a trained warrior or military leader, his reaction to God's call suggests he's anything but. His skills may reside in growing crops or raising animals, not commanding an army and defeating the enemy.

Given this assumption, his reluctance seems warranted. A farmer can't lead an army and prevail against a stronger foe—at least not from a human standpoint. But with God, all things are possible. God even promises victory.

Still, Barak is unwilling to obey—unless Deborah goes with him. As you may recall in the chapter on Aaron, Moses did the same thing when God called him. And God sent him Aaron to help.

With Deborah at his side, Barak finally obeys. Their army prevails, just as God promised. Then Deborah and Barak sing a song of praise to God.

In this story, we see Deborah as brave, while Barak comes across as a coward. Yet the book of Hebrews affirms Barak for his faith and doesn't list Deborah.

Though we may perceive Barak as a man who lacks courage, God sees him as a man of noteworthy faith.

How do we react when God calls us to do something we feel unqualified to do? Do we let our faith override logic or allow logic to control us?

[Read about Barak in Judges 4–5. Discover more in Hebrews 11:32–34.]

89. JAEL

Deborah prophesied that the credit for killing the enemy commander, Sisera, would go to a woman. We may assume Deborah is that woman. She's not.

When Barak and Deborah lead the Israelite army and rout Sisera's forces, the enemy commander escapes. He takes refuge with a woman named Jael because her family has a connection with his country.

Jael offers him sanctuary, gives him something to drink, and stands guard at the tent opening so he can rest. Her protection is a ruse. Once he falls asleep, she drives a tent peg through his temple. Though gruesome, it may be the only means she has to kill him. She's brave enough to act and strong enough to pierce his skull.

This fulfills Deborah's prophecy.

As a tribute to Jael's valor, Deborah and Barak immortalize her actions in a song of praise.

Are the things we do worth singing about? Will future generations hear about what we do for God?

[Read about Jael in Judges 4:17–22 and 5:24–27. Discover another person who people sang about in 1 Samuel 18:5-7.]

90. GIDEON

Gideon is an interesting judge. The Bible gives us three chapters about key events in his life. Some of what he does inspires us and provides an example to follow. Yet he does other things we should certainly avoid. But aren't we all like that, with both strengths and weaknesses?

In our first story Gideon is threshing wheat in a winepress. If this seems weird, that's because it is. But he's afraid of having his grain stolen by the Midianites, so he's working in an unlikely place where they may not notice him. Then God's angel shows up, addresses him as a mighty warrior, and tells him to go in his own strength to save his people. Gideon questions the angel, and God's emissary must prove himself to the fearful man.

After doing so, he tells Gideon to destroy his father's altar to Baal. Gideon does, but he does so at night for fear of the townspeople. When they find out what he did, they want to kill him, but his father intercedes and stops them.

We best know Gideon, however, for putting out a fleece to determine God's will. Although Gideon has already marshaled an army to attack his enemy, he asks God if he will prevail, even though the Almighty has already promised he will.

Gideon's test is simple. He'll lay a ball of wool—a fleece—on the ground. If the morning dew falls only on the wool and not the ground, Gideon will conclude he'll be victorious. The next morning the wool is dripping wet. The surrounding area is dry.

Yet Gideon doubts. He repeats the test, this time requesting the opposite outcome. The next morning, the wool is dry and the ground, wet. At this second confirmation, he believes God.

Many have followed Gideon's example of "putting out a fleece" to determine God's will. Yet we should note that God doesn't tell us to do this. Instead, the Bible merely describes what Gideon did, without commenting on the wisdom of doing so.

This story shows both Gideon's lack of confidence in God and the Almighty's patience with his doubtful servant.

Next, God tells Gideon his army of 32,000 is too big. The people will see the victory and assume they did it on their own. God desires a smaller force to prove his hand in the outcome. Whittling the army down to three hundred, Gideon moves forward in confident faith to victory, which God orchestrates.

After this, the people want to make Gideon their king. He declines, reminding them that God is their king.

Yet, after this wise response, Gideon foolishly collects a gold earring from each man's plunder. He uses this to make a golden ephod (a ceremonial garment), which the people worship instead of God.

Though Gideon at times acts with bravery, faith, and wisdom, he also doubts, tests God, and makes a foolish decision, which mark his legacy.

In what ways are we like Gideon? What lessons can we learn from his life?

[Read about Gideon in Judges 6–8. Discover more in Hebrews 11:32–34.]

91. ABIMELEK (2)

bimelek is the son of Gideon (also called Jerub-Baal). The Bible first lists Abimelek's mother as Gideon's concubine and later as his slave. Either way, the boy has a less-than-ideal start to life. But this does not excuse his behavior as an adult. He could have risen above the circumstances of his birth. But, as we will soon see, he does not.

Abimelek has seventy half-brothers. Yes, seventy. This means Gideon fathered children with many women. Abimelek goes to Shechem, where his mother is from, and asks if they want him to rule them—as one of their own—or if they want Gideon's seventy sons. The people choose him and give him money.

Abimelek uses the funds to raise an army of "reckless scoundrels." He returns home to Ophrah, where he murders his half-brothers. Only the youngest, Jotham (1), escapes.

The people of Shechem make Abimelek their king.

After three years, God causes a rift between Abimelek and the people. He does this to bring about the punishment of Abimelek for murdering his brothers—and the people of Shechem for their indirect role.

A man named Gaal moves to Shechem. He opposes Abimelek.

The two go into battle, with Gaal leading the people of Shechem against Abimelek and his hired army. Abimelek prevails. The next day, he takes revenge on the town of Shechem. He kills all the people. Since all his mother's relatives live there, he presumably kills them too. He destroys the city.

Then Abimelek attacks the city of Thebez. He besieges it and captures it. Inside the city, the people flee to a tower. As Abimelek approaches the stronghold to burn it and the people inside, a woman drops an upper millstone. It hits Abimelek and cracks his skull.

Lest it be said a woman killed him, Abimelek instructs his armor-bearer to run him through. The servant does.

Abimelek dies having done nothing positive in his life. He leaves a legacy of evil, having caused the death of many—and himself.

How can we rise above our past to make a better future for ourselves and others? What sort of legacy are we leaving?

[Read about Abimelek in Judges 9. Discover more about Shechem in Genesis 34.]

92. JOTHAM (1)

When Abimelek returns home to murder his seventy brothers, only Jotham, the youngest one, survives. He hides to escape execution.

When Jotham learns the people of Shechem have made his half-brother their king, he climbs a mountain. From this lofty position, he shouts to them.

He shares a story about trees looking for a king to rule over them. Each one they ask, declines. At last, the thornbush agrees.

In doing so, he implies that Abimelek is the thornbush, as well as the least desirable choice as Shechem's ruler.

Then Jotham criticizes their foolishness in making Abimelek king instead of letting his brothers continue their father Gideon's legacy.

To conclude, Jotham proclaims curses on Abimelek for the murder of his brothers and on Shechem for helping.

Then he flees and hides in fear. This is the last we hear of Jotham.

Scripture concludes the pathetic tale of Abimelek's life noting this was how God punished the evil man for killing his brothers, as well as destroying the wicked city of Shechem for facilitating it.

This fulfills Jotham's curse.

What do we think about Jotham pronouncing a curse on Abimelek? What is an area where we should proclaim truth like Jotham?

[Read about Jotham in Judges 9:5–21. Discover more in Judges 9:56–57.]

93. GAAL

We know nothing about Gaal except what appears in this passage in the book of Judges. Though the text often mentions him as the son of Ebed, Scripture tells us nothing about his father either.

What we do know is that Gaal moves with his family to the town of Shechem. This is during the time of Abimelek's rule. Gaal earns the town's respect, and they put their trust in him. During the grape harvest, they hold a festival, eating and drinking in celebration. It's then that the people—perhaps inebriated—curse Abimelek.

Gaal builds on their dissatisfaction and questions Abimelek's fitness to rule. "If only I had an army," Gaal muses, "I would get rid of him."

The townspeople rally behind Gaal's leadership and go out with him to fight.

But Zebul, the governor of Shechem, warns Abimelek of Gaal's coup attempt. Abimelek is ready and defeats Gaal's army, killing many.

Zebul drives Gaal and his family out of Shechem. The troublemaker is gone.

When have we gone some place new and tried to change it? What was the outcome?

[Read about Gaal in Judges 9:26–41. Discover a comparable situation in 2 Samuel 15:1–4.]

94. JEPHTHAH

Jephthah is the son of Gilead and a prostitute. Gilead and his wife have other sons, who drive Jephthah away, lest they must share their inheritance with him. Jephthah forms a gang of troublemakers.

Some time later, the Ammonites fight Israel. In desperation, the elders of Gilead ask Jephthah to lead them into battle. He agrees, but then makes a rash vow.

Jephthah pledges that upon his successful return he will sacrifice the first thing that comes through the door of his house as a burnt offering to thank God for his victory. Jephthah assumes it will be an animal.

He is indeed victorious.

To his dismay, the first thing that walks through the door when he returns home is his daughter. She dances in celebration for his success. She is his only child. He laments the foolish promise he made to God but feels obligated to fulfill it.

We don't know the name of Jephthah's daughter, but we do grieve her fate. She doesn't complain about her father's careless promise. Instead, she confirms he must follow through. Her only request is a two-month reprieve to mourn her misfortune with her friends. We applaud her steadfast confidence in how she accepts her father's pledge, revealing her deep faith in God.

Then Jephthah follows through on his vow.

What's unclear is if Jephthah physically sacrifices his daughter, something Moses prohibited, or if her life is redeemed for service to God, like Hannah will later do in giving her son Samuel to serve God in the temple.

Regardless, it's clear that Jephthah's daughter will not enjoy the future she expected, for she willingly accepts the consequences of her father's impulsive vow to God. We commend her for her pious attitude, all the while being reminded to be careful with what we promise.

When have we made a rash vow? Whether we followed through or reneged, what do we feel about our response to our unwise promise?

[Read about Jephthah in Judges 11. Discover more in the story of Hannah and Samuel in 1 Samuel 1:10–22.]

95. MICAH (1)

hough Micah appears in the book of Judges, we'd be wrong to consider him a judge. He never judged or led the people. In fact, the Bible doesn't record a single good thing he does. Here's an overview:

Micah steals eleven hundred shekels of silver from his mother. Not knowing who the robber is, she curses the person who took her money.

When Micah reveals himself as the thief, she in turn blesses him. She consecrates the silver to the Lord and commissions a silversmith to make an idol. This is precisely what she shouldn't do with silver she dedicated to God, but she does.

Micah puts the idol in a shrine he had made. The shrine also contains an ephod and other idols. One of his sons serves as priest.

When a Levite from Bethlehem happens by, Micah installs him as priest and provides for him. Never mind that a Levite isn't supposed to serve as a priest, especially not at a shrine of idols. But this Levite doesn't care. He just wants a place to stay and to do something he feels is important.

Some spies from the tribe of Dan stop by. They're on a mission.

They inquire of the priest about their journey. He gives them God's approval and sends them away in peace.

Later the spies return with an army, intent on conquering a nearby city. They take Micah's idol, his ephod, and his household gods. They talk Micah's priest into going with them. Micah chases them but later gives up when he realizes he'll lose.

The army from Dan conquers the city and burns it. Then they rebuild it and settle there. They worship the idol Micah made.

Everything in the story of Micah is contrary to the laws of Moses and disrespects the Lord. This is Micah's legacy.

What conclusions can we draw from Micah's mom proclaiming both a curse and a blessing? What have we consecrated or dedicated to the Lord?

[Read about Micah in Judges 17–18. Discover another dedication in Judges 16:17.]

96. SAMSON

A nother judge is Samson. His story begins even before his birth. An angel appears to a childless woman and tells her she'll become pregnant and have a son. The angel says the boy will be dedicated to God, even before he is born.

He then gives the woman special dietary expectations. Though we may assume these only apply while she's pregnant, the text suggests they continue after his birth. The boy, who is to be a Nazirite, also has rules to follow, such as never cutting his hair.

What a grand start to life: dedicated to God even before birth.

Yet Samson fails to live up to the Almighty's expectations for his life. He squanders his great beginning. Though God does use him to kill some of the nation's Philistine enemies, this isn't because of Samson's right behavior. Instead, God uses Samson despite his faulty character. He disrespects his parents, disobeys God, and doesn't control his sexual desires.

Samson touches a carcass, though God prohibits it. Samson also likes foreign women, also contrary to God's law. He marries a Philistine woman, but the seven-day wedding celebration doesn't go well. It's all because he challenged thirty of the men in attendance with a riddle.

They can't solve it and press his bride for the solution. She doesn't know and plies Samson for the answer. With constant tears and pleading, she wears him down and he explains it to her. She tells the thirty men, and they answer the riddle, winning the bet Samson made with them. To pay up, Samson kills thirty other men, takes their clothes, and gives them to the men at the wedding.

Then Samson abandons his new wife, and her father gives her to another. When Samson wants her back, it's too late. In retaliation, he burns their crops. The Philistines blame the woman and her father for this and kill them. Samson escalates the conflict further, slaying many more in revenge.

Another time Samson hires a prostitute.

Later he falls in love with Delilah. She proves to be his undoing.

The Philistines hire Delilah to uncover the source of Samson's strength so they can capture him and stop him from killing more of their people.

She asks him to share his secret with her and he toys with her, giving false information, but each time he edges closer to the truth. He eventually reveals that the secret to his strength is that he's never had a haircut.

She calls for the Philistines to shave his head. Then they capture him. They gouge his eyes and throw him in prison.

His hair begins to grow back, and he asks God for one final burst of strength. God grants his request, and Samson destroys the Philistine temple by taking out one of its main supports. The building crumbles, killing 3,000 Philistines and Samson along with them.

Whether little or much, have we made the most of the start we've been given in life? When we make mistakes, do we believe God can still use us?

[Read about Samson in Judges 13–16. Discover more in Hebrews 11:32–34.]

97. DELILAH

Delilah is infamous for her tryst with bad-boy Samson, but we know little more about her. The Bible says Samson falls in love with her, but we don't know if it's reciprocal. She may have had other reasons to pursue a relationship with him.

Whatever her initial motivation to hook up with the powerful Samson, money soon becomes a greater incentive. The Philistine leaders offer her silver if she can uncover the secret behind her lover's immense strength. She agrees.

Eager to earn her reward, she plies Samson to reveal the source of his vigor. Three times he toys with her, giving misinformation, which she accepts as truth. Each time the Philistines use this information to try to capture him. Each time they fail.

Humiliated by her inability to learn the truth, and eager to earn her payout, she badgers him. Her nagging eventually wears him down. He breaks and reveals everything to her.

Now knowing the true secret to his might, the Philistines cut his hair. Then they capture him since he now lacks the strength to escape.

Whatever Delilah thought of Samson at first, she readily sold him out for a sack of silver.

What are we willing to do to make money? Do we put wealth, power, or prestige ahead of our relationships with others—and with God?

[Read about Delilah in Judges 16:4–21. Discover another person motivated by money in Matthew 26:14–16.]

98. ELIMELEK

During the time of the judges, we come across a man named Elimelek. Scripture tells us little about him, covering his story in a scant three verses.

He's married to Naomi, and they have two sons. They live in Bethlehem, which is part of Judah. There's a famine, so they head off to Moab. There Elimelek dies.

His sons both get married, one to Orpah and the other to Ruth. Then they die too.

This leaves widowed Naomi with no sons and two daughters-in-law. We'll cover them in the next few chapters.

Elimelek's life seems like a most unremarkable one. He marries, has two kids, and struggles to make a living. Then he dies.

It's depressing.

But there's more to his story. Though Elimelek dies without having done anything noteworthy in his life, he does play an essential role in Jesus's family tree. Had he not taken his family to Moab, Jesus wouldn't have been born. The following chapters, building up to Ruth, will explain.

Though we all want to make the most of our life and impact our world, we may not see the results we want. Yet our influence can continue after we're gone.

Are we making the most of our life in how we live each day? Do we believe God can use the things we do now to define the future?

[Read about Elimelek in Ruth 1:1–3. Discover another family that moved because of a famine in Genesis 47:20.]

99. NAOMI

Naomi's name means *pleasant*.

Naomi, her husband, and their two boys leave their home in Judah because of a famine. They travel to Moab in search of food. While in this foreign land, Naomi's husband dies. Later, both of her married sons die too. This leaves her with two widowed daughters-in-law, Orpah and Ruth, and little hope.

Naomi blames God for her misfortune and grows resentful. She even tries to change her name to Mara, which means "bitter."

Naomi decides to return home when she hears they have food there. Orpah and Ruth head back with her, but Naomi decides this isn't fair to them. At Naomi's urging, Orpah returns to Moab to rejoin her family, but Ruth insists on staying with her mother-in-law.

Once in Juda, Naomi devises a strategy for Ruth to marry their relative, Boaz. Ruth follows her mother-in-law's instructions exactly as directed, and events play out as Naomi hopes. Boaz and Ruth soon marry. Ruth has her first child, Obed. Naomi cares for her new grandson like a son, while the local women celebrate his birth and Naomi's good fortune.

Naomi's life—like everyone's life—contains both struggle and disappointment, but God cares for her. He provides a loyal daughter-in-law and a cherished grandson, her first.

Even if life goes terribly wrong and we become bitter against God, criticizing him for our troubles, he still loves us and provides for us.

Do we trust God with our future, regardless of the situation? Have we ever blamed God for our misfortune?

[Read about Naomi throughout Ruth 1–4. Discover more about bitterness in Hebrews 12:15 and James 3:14.]

100. MAHLON AND KILION

Mahlon and Kilion are the sons of Elimelek and Naomi. During the time of the judges, there's a famine. In search of food, the family moves from Bethlehem to Moab and settles there.

Elimelek dies in Moab. Mahlon and Kilion marry local Moabite girls. Mahlon marries Ruth, and Kilion marries Orpah.

Both Mahlon and Kilion die in Moab too. As a result, all three women are widows—and destitute.

Naomi and Ruth head back to Bethlehem, while Orpah stays in Moab.

It's in Bethlehem that Boaz marries Ruth, who becomes the great-grandmother of King David and ancestor of Jesus.

Had Mahlon and Kilion not died, Naomi and Ruth would have stayed in Moab and Boaz would have never met and married Ruth. It may, however, be an overstretch to say that God caused Mahlon and Kilion's death to accomplish his will.

God, however, does work all things together for good to those who love him and are called to his purpose (Romans 8:28). With this in mind, we can see how the Almighty uses this situation to unite Ruth with Boaz, which otherwise would not have happened.

When a loved one dies, do we blame God? When have we seen our Lord work things out for good in our lives?

[Read about Mahlon and Kilion in Ruth 1:1–5. Discover more in Ruth 4:9–10.]

101. ORPAH

O rpah is the widowed daughter-in-law of Naomi and the sister-in-law of Ruth.

When Naomi heads for home, she encourages Orpah and Ruth to stay behind. Though Ruth refuses, Orpah does the logical thing and returns.

That's the last we hear of her.

We don't know if she marries again or ever has children. We don't know how long she lives. We just know she did the sensible thing.

Orpah's sister-in-law, however, chooses the path that doesn't make sense, and God honors her for her loyalty to him and her mother-in-law.

Sometimes the sensible solution isn't the one God honors.

Who are we loyal to and why? Do we put God first even when it doesn't make sense?

[Read about Orpah in Ruth 1:4–14. Discover more about putting God first in Proverbs 3:5–6 and Matthew 22:36–38.]

102. RUTH

Ruth is a widow. She's a foreigner; that is, she's not a Hebrew. And she remains faithful to Naomi, her mother-in-law, also a widow.

Here's Ruth's story.

When Naomi returns home to Judah from Moab, she urges Ruth to stay behind in her own country, with her own family. Ruth, however, won't consider it. She clings to her mother-in-law and pledges her allegiance to Naomi and to Naomi's God.

We can only guess at the reason behind Ruth's intense loyalty to Naomi. Having lost her husband and both sons, Naomi has become a bitter woman, so it certainly isn't her shining character that prompts Ruth's devotion.

When they return to Judah, Ruth searches for grain missed by the harvesters so that she and Naomi will have some food to eat. In doing so Ruth puts herself in a dangerous situation, should a harvester harass or take advantage of her. Yet Ruth ends up in the fields of a wealthy farmer, Boaz. He's heard of her devotion to Naomi and appreciates her hardworking nature and godly character. She finds favor with him, and he promises her protection when she's in his fields.

Naomi wants to find another husband for Ruth.

Although older, Boaz seems the ideal choice, since he's a close relative, a kinsman who can redeem her through marriage, as prescribed in the Law of Moses (Leviticus 25:25). Naomi develops a shrewd strategy for Ruth to go to Boaz at night and capture his attention. Ruth dutifully does as her mother-in-law directs. While it's unclear if Naomi's instructions cause Ruth to act in a manner considered brazen, she does gain Boaz's notice.

When Boaz and Ruth marry, the people bless her and her future children.

Ruth has her first child, a boy they name Obed. Obed is the father of Jesse, the father of David. This makes Ruth the great-grandmother of King David.

God rewards Ruth's allegiance to him and loyalty to her mother-in-law, providing Ruth with a husband, saving her from poverty, and giving her a son.

Ruth is one of four women honored by Matthew in his record of Jesus's family tree. She is his direct ancestor.

Do we have a reputation for being loyal and hardworking? Is our godly character affirmed by others?

[Read about Ruth in Ruth 1–4. Discover more in Matthew 1:1–5.]

103. BOAZ

Boaz is a wealthy farmer living in Judah. He was a close relative of the Elimelek we covered a few chapters ago. Boaz is also a respected man, well known for his integrity.

When Ruth goes out to glean the grain the harvesters missed, she ends up in one of Boaz's fields. He knows her by reputation, but this is the first time he sees her. Boaz approaches. He affirms her loyalty to Naomi, promises her safety in his fields, and gives her the same privileges as his laborers—even though she is but a poor widow scavenging for food.

Excited to learn that Ruth ended up in Boaz's field and favorably interacted with him, Naomi later sends Ruth to the threshing floor at night to get Boaz's attention. Ruth asks him to redeem her. In effect, she's asking him to marry her. It's a proposal of sorts.

Attracted to her, Boaz is willing, but he isn't her closest relative. Another man is. Boaz can only marry Ruth if the other man declines to do so.

Boaz immediately sets out to make Ruth his wife, deftly dealing with the other relative who could thwart his intentions.

They marry and have a baby boy. Though we don't know if Boaz has other children, this is Ruth's first.

They name him Obed. He is the grandfather of King David and a direct ancestor of Jesus.

One more thing. Remember Rahab, the prostitute who helped the spies? She's Boaz's mother.

Do people affirm us as someone with integrity? How do we treat those who are less fortunate than we are?

[Read about Boaz in Ruth 2–4. Discover more in Matthew 1:1–5.]

104. OBED (1)

O bed is Boaz and Ruth's first son. Though Ruth was first married to Mahlon, they had no children. The Bible doesn't mention Boaz and Ruth having any more children, so Obed may be an only child.

The women in the village praise God for Obed's birth. They bless him and proclaim that he will become famous throughout the land. Though we don't know if Obed himself becomes famous, we do know that his grandson—King David—becomes well known and a man after God's own heart (1 Samuel 13:14 and Acts 13:22). David indeed becomes famous.

And Jesus descends from Obed many centuries later. Jesus is even more famous.

What are we known for? What can we do to prepare our children to do amazing things for God?

[Read about Obed in Ruth 4:13–22. Discover more in Matthew 1:5.]

105. JABEZ

Though an entire book was later written about his brief prayer, we know little about Jabez from Scripture. The Bible only mentions him in two obscure verses, buried in a lengthy genealogy.

We know his birth is difficult, and the name his mother gives him reflects the physical pain his arrival caused.

We also know that Jabez is an honorable man, more honorable than others. And he has a deep connection with God, for when he prays a bold prayer, God answers it.

What is his prayer? It has five components:

1. Bless me (so that I may be a blessing to others).

2. Enlarge my territory (which increases my influence).

3. May your hand guide me (for I'd be foolish to try anything on my own).

4. Keep me from harm (that is, keep me safe).

5. Spare me from pain (that is, save me from suffering).

After Jabez makes his bold request, God says, "Yes!"

How well do we do at praying bold prayers? What do we think about adapting Jabez's prayer as our own?

[Read about Jabez in 1 Chronicles 4:9–10. Discover another answered prayer in Judges 16:28–30.]

106. ELKANAH (4)

Elkanah, from the tribe of Ephriam, has two wives. They are Hannah and Peninnah. Having two wives is never a smart idea. Conflict is sure to result. Such is the case between Elkanah's two wives.

The text says Elkanah loves Hannah. The implication is that he does not love Peninnah. Or at least he does not love her as much. This escalates the tension between the two women.

Peninnah has many children, but Hannah has none. Peninnah torments the childless Hannah. Though Elkanah is aware of how Peninnah treats Hannah, he does nothing to protect her or stop the harassment.

His attitude is that he should be more important to her than even ten sons. In saying this he shows how highly he thinks of himself and how little he thinks of Hannah's longing to have a son.

If we're married, how well do we understand our spouse's feelings and desires? When we see one person treating another unfairly, do we ignore the situation or intervene?

[Read about Elkanah in 1 Samuel 1:1–8. Discover more in 1 Samuel 1:21–23.]

107. HANNAH

Hannah, married to Elkanah, longs to have a son but is childless. Adding to her misery, everyone harasses her. Though she's her husband's favorite wife, he dismisses her infertility. He fails to protect her from the verbal assaults of his other wife, Peninnah, who torments her.

When Hannah prays earnestly, Eli, the priest, accuses her of being drunk. But she's in deep despair over her childless condition and challenging home life.

Hannah cries out to God in anguish, begging him to give her a son. She asks for a boy, not just a child. If God will answer her request, she promises to give the boy to God for a lifetime of service.

God understands Hannah, even though Elkanah, Peninnah, and Eli fail her. The Lord hears her plea and gives her a son.

Hannah names the boy Samuel, saying, "because I asked the Lord for him."

After weaning Samuel, Hannah gives him to Eli for a lifetime of service to God at the temple, just as she promised. When Hannah and her family make their pilgrimage to the temple to offer their sacrifices to God each year, she sees young Samuel and gives him a new robe.

God blesses Hannah with five more children.

As with Hannah, God understands our situation, even when no one else does.

Will we trust God to rescue us from our turmoil? When we make a promise to the Lord, do we follow through and do as we say?

[Read about Hannah in 1 Samuel 1:1–28 and 1 Samuel 2:19–21. Discover more in 1 Samuel 2:1–11.]

108. PENINNAH

Peninnah is a co-wife with Hannah. They're both married to Elkanah.

Reminiscent of Jacob and his two wives, Rachel and Leah, we have the story of Elkanah and his two wives, Hannah and Peninnah. Just as Jacob loves Rachel more than Leah, Elkanah loves Hannah more than Peninnah. Likewise, as Rachel, the favored wife, is childless, so, too, is Hannah.

Another parallel biblical account is of Abraham, Sarah, and Hagar, where Hagar, the wife with a child, harasses Sarah, the wife without one. So too, Peninnah harasses Hannah.

Despite Peninnah producing children for Elkanah, he loves Hannah. Peninnah lashes out by verbally harassing Hannah. Though we shouldn't condone what Peninnah does, we can understand her actions. But that doesn't make what she does right.

When we're in a trying situation, do we seek to make the best of it or harass others? When have we risen above an unfair situation in a God-honoring way?

[Read about Peninnah in 1 Samuel 1:1–6. Discover parallel situations in Genesis 16:1–16 and Genesis 29:14–35.]

109. SAMUEL (1)

Those who grew up hearing Bible stories may remember the account of young Samuel. He is the son of Elkanah and Hannah. His mother takes him to live at the temple and help Eli, the priest. Each year she visits him and gives him a little robe to wear. You may even recall a picture of the bright-eyed Samuel smiling as his mother gives him his new outfit.

This idyllic scene ignores the fact that Hannah commits Samuel to a lifetime of service before he is born; he has no say in the matter. This also requires him to leave his home to live with a stranger, a man who wasn't a good father to his own sons. How distraught young Samuel must have been over being separated from his mother and having his entire future planned for him.

Yet Samuel excels in this environment. As a young boy he can hear the voice of God, something few others can do in that day.

Though Eli is a priest, Samuel lacks the bloodline (a descendant of Aaron) to succeed him as priest. When Eli dies, however, Samuel replaces him as the leader of all Israel. The Bible also calls Samuel a prophet (a seer).

Up to this time, Israel did not have a king. God served as their king. And he used a series of judges to rescue his wayward people from their enemies and return their focus to him each time they fell away.

When Samuel grows older, he appoints his sons to take over for him. But they are corrupt, just like the sons of his mentor. Samuel must've learned his parenting skills from the inept Eli.

The elders go to Samuel and ask him to appoint a king to rule over the nation. This distresses Samuel, but the Almighty tells him it's okay. The people aren't rejecting Samuel's leadership; they're rejecting God's. Although reluctant, Samuel anoints Saul to be Israel's first king, as directed by the Lord. When Saul later falters, God tells Samuel to anoint David to replace Saul.

How do we react when we end up in a situation we didn't choose? Whether our position is grand or humble, do we serve God to the best of our abilities, like Samuel?

[Read about Samuel in 1 Samuel 1–25. Discover more in Hebrews 11:32–34.]

110. HOPHNI AND PHINEHAS (2)

Hophni and Phinehas are priests, just like their father Eli. Hophni and Phinehas, however, do not behave as proper priests should.

When the people come to offer their sacrifices, Hophni and Phinehas fail to respect the offerings or handle them as prescribed by Moses. In doing so they show contempt for the gifts the people make to God. Furthermore, Hophni and Phinehas sleep with the women who serve at the tent of meeting.

Eli hears about what his sons are doing and confronts them, trying to get them to change their evil behavior. But his sons don't listen to their father's attempt to correct their actions. They continue doing what they've always done.

One of the Lord's prophets comes to Eli with a harsh rebuke from God. Because of their wickedness, the prophet foretells that Hophni and Phinehas will both die on the same day. In their place, God will provide a new priest, a faithful leader.

Though we may think this new priest alludes to the young boy Samuel, Samuel never becomes a priest (though he does become a great prophet). Samuel can't become a priest because he's not a descendant of Aaron. Instead, this prophecy looks forward to the priesthood of Jesus, anointed to minister forever.

As prophesied, Hophni and Phinehas both die on the same day. In doing so, God ends their wickedness.

How do we respond when God convicts us of our wrong actions? Do we think that, because of God's mercy, we can ignore what he tells us to do?

[Read about Hophni and Phinehas in 1 Samuel 2:12–36. Discover more in 1 Samuel 4:2–11.]

111. ELI

Eli is a priest. He serves the Lord for forty years. When Eli grows older, his two boys, Hophni and Phinehas, take over the daily priestly duties for him, as prescribed by Moses.

While we can assume Eli is a good priest, his boys are not. Scripture says so. When Eli tries to correct his sons' improper behavior as priests, they dismiss his warning.

Though they are adults and responsible for their own actions, the disrespect they show for their father suggests he may have failed to raise them right. Regardless, they surely don't respect what Eli tells them, just as they don't respect God's commands for how they should conduct themselves as priests.

A prophet comes to Eli prophesying that, because of their wickedness, Hophni and Phinehas will die on the same day.

Not only do they die as foretold, but the Philistines also capture the ark of God. When Eli hears the news, he falls backward in his chair, breaks his neck, and dies.

How do the actions of our children (or those under our authority) reflect on us? Will God judge us accordingly if we don't lead our family (or our charges) well?

[Read about Eli in 1 Samuel 2:22–25 and 1 Samuel 4:12–18. Discover more in 1 Kings 2:27.]

DAVID, A MAN AFTER GOD'S OWN HEART

Though God intended to lead his people, they clamor for a king to reign over them like all the other nations. At God's direction, Samuel reluctantly gives them one. The first king is Saul. When he doesn't work out, God picks a second one, David, despite the man's shortcomings. Nevertheless, the Bible calls him a man after God's own heart (1 Samuel 13:14 and Acts 13:22).

With the kingship establishing God's people as a nation, we'll explore some of the kings and prophets who follow David. Eventually their repeated disobedience receives God's punishment, which occurs when they're conquered and deported.

But to set the stage for this, we'll first consider King Saul.

112. SAUL (1)

S aul is the first king of Israel.

God directs Samuel, the prophet, to anoint Saul when the people ask for a human king to rule over them instead of God. Saul is a head taller than everyone else and handsome too. From a physical perspective, he's a smart choice. After Samuel anoints him as king, God's Spirit comes upon Saul, and he prophesies. What a promising start for God's first king.

A few days later, Samuel gathers the nation to publicly declare Saul as king. Yet when the time comes, they can't find Saul. He's hiding. We can only guess if he disappears out of fear or if he doesn't want the job. Regardless, his actions suggest that Saul may not turn out to be a good king.

Some time later, Saul gathers his army to fight the Philistines who have come against them. Samuel tells Saul to wait seven days for him so he can come to offer a burnt offering to the Lord and seek his favor. Then Saul can engage in battle.

Saul waits one week, but Samuel doesn't arrive. The army begins to desert, and the king grows anxious. He takes it upon himself to offer the sacrifice.

Just when he finishes, Samuel shows up and rebukes the king for his disobedience. Though God had planned to establish Saul's kingdom forever, God rejects him as king because of Saul's sin, pledging to give the kingdom to another, a man after God's own heart.

Then Samuel anoints David as king. However, David does not ascend to the throne right away, and Saul continues to rule, even though God has left him.

After Samuel dies, Saul is desperate for supernatural guidance, but God is silent. Saul goes to an outlawed medium and asks her to consult the spirit of Samuel. Samuel, irritated at having his idyllic afterlife disturbed, delivers disheartening news to Saul. He prophesies that the Philistines will defeat Israel, with Saul and his sons dying in battle.

This is exactly what happens.

Is our character worthy of what God calls us to do? When God seems distant or remains silent, do we resort to inappropriate spiritual practices?

[Read about Saul throughout 1 Samuel 9–11, 13–28, and 31. Discover more in 2 Samuel 21:1–14.]

113. JONATHAN (3)

Jonathan is the son of King Saul and next in line to the throne. Though Saul's plan is for Jonathan to succeed him, Jonathan sees God's perspective instead. The heir apparent realizes that David is to be the next king and not him. Jonathan accepts this.

Though there could be animosity between Jonathan and David, the pair enjoy a close relationship, with Jonathan pledging his support for David's future rule.

Another demonstration of Jonathan's character and faith in God comes at a time when Israel's army is outmatched and in despair. Only Saul and Jonathan have swords, while the rest of the army have makeshift weapons.

Jonathan and his armor-bearer sneak away from camp and boldly attack a Philistine outpost. Though Jonathan isn't confident in a victory, he knows God *can* bring it about.

With only one sword, Jonathan and his young armor-bearer kill twenty Philistines. God sends a panic throughout the enemy camp, and they scatter. The Israelite army pursues them and wins a great battle against a more powerful foe.

Through God, one person can make a difference.

Are we willing to accept God's plan for our future when it opposes our families' or friends' expectations? Are we a person God can use to make a difference?

[Read about Jonathan in 1 Samuel 13–14, 18–20, and 23. Discover more in 1 Samuel 31:2.]

114. JESSE

In most of the instances when Jesse appears in Scripture, it's in relation to his son David, as in "David, son of Jesse," or simply "the son of Jesse."

Yet the first time we encounter Jesse in the Bible, this is not the case. Here's what happens:

God has rejected Saul as king and tasks Samuel to appoint a new one. The Lord directs Samuel to go to Jesse in the town of Bethlehem. There Samuel is to anoint one of Jesse's sons as king. God doesn't tell Samuel which boy to pick, merely that he'll indicate which one when the time comes.

When Samuel sees Jesse's oldest son, Eliab, the prophet assumes he is the one God wants. But he is not. Neither is Jesse's second son, Abinadab, nor the third son, Shammah.

Jesse presents all seven of his boys to Samuel, but God doesn't pick any of them. When Samuel presses Jesse, he admits he has one more son, David, who's out tending the sheep. It's as if Jesse forgot David. Surely, he dismissed his youngest son as not being worthy.

But God sees things differently than Jesse and differently than we do. He directs Samuel to anoint David as king. The least of Jesse's sons will become the greatest.

When have we dismissed any of our family or friends, failing to see them as God sees them? When has God surprised us by who he picked to serve him?

[Read about Jesse in 1 Samuel 16:1–13. Discover more in 1 Samuel 17:12–18.]

115. DAVID (1)

D avid, the shepherd boy turned king, shows up in Scripture more than any other Old Testament character. Even the New Testament mentions him often. He appears in twenty-eight of the Bible's sixty-six books, with more than nine hundred mentions.

It's enough content for an entire book, with much we can learn from David and much God can teach us.

David, however, is best known for two events in his life: one a triumph and the other a failure.

The first story comes from early in his life when he kills the huge warrior Goliath. He takes down this giant of a man using only a slingshot and a single stone. But the projectile doesn't kill Goliath, it only knocks him out. David runs to the fallen Philistine hero and pulls out the man's own sword. David uses it to kill him and then cut off his head.

David's time spent protecting his father's sheep from wild animals prepared him for this moment, but his faith in God gave him the victory.

The other well-known incident in David's life is when he commits adultery with the beautiful Bathsheba.

He sees her. He wants her. He takes her. It doesn't matter that he already has several wives, and she already has a husband.

She gets pregnant.

To cover the pregnancy, David calls back her husband, Uriah, from the front lines and tries twice to reunite him with his wife for the night. When this strategy fails, David sends Uriah back to the front lines along with a message for the commander. The communiqué is a plan to ensure Uriah's death.

The plan succeeds. David marries Bathsheba, but their baby dies.

From a moral perspective, this is the lowest point in David's life. He commits adultery and murder. Yet David repents to restore his relationship with God.

A third element of David's life, however, stands out as even more noteworthy. When Samuel confronts King Saul for his disobedience, Samuel confirms that Saul's kingdom will end, and another will replace him. Samuel says that God has sought a man after his own heart and appointed him to rule the people. This man is David.

Much later, Paul confirms this fact when speaking to the people in Pisidian Antioch, stating that God said, "I've found David, a man after my own heart. He'll do everything I want him to do."

Twice, the Bible refers to David as a man after God's own heart. This may be the highest honor anyone could ever receive.

Are we a person after God's own heart? What might we do to move closer to this outcome?

[Read about David in 1 Samuel 16 to 2 Samuel 24. Discover more in Acts 13:22.]

116. GOLIATH

Even though Scripture contains only one story about Goliath, most people know it well. This, however, is not for his valor but for his arrogance.

Goliath serves in the Philistine army. He stands out because he's taller than everyone else. His stature is an amazing nine feet.

The Israelite army squares off against the Philistine army, with a valley separating them. Each morning Goliath comes out and taunts them. He challenges them to send out their champion to fight. Whichever man loses, their nation will become subject to the other.

As a large man with a formidable appearance, Goliath is confident of victory.

The Israelite army cowers in fear before this imposing man. No one dares to fight him. No one, that is, until young David comes along.

Full of godly confidence, David runs toward the arrogant Goliath with only his sling and five stones. Goliath mocks him for his audacity.

Yet with David slinging his first stone, Goliath falls. David uses the giant-of-a-man's own sword to behead him.

With their defeated champion lying dead in the valley, the

Philistine army flees. The Israelite army gives pursuit. They rout their enemy and plunder their camp.

From a human standpoint, Goliath stands as the sure victor. Yet David prevails. Such is the case when we align ourselves with the Lord Almighty.

With God on our side, one person can make the difference.

Are we more like Goliath or like David? How well do we do at placing our confidence in God instead of our own abilities?

[Read about Goliath in 1 Samuel 17:1–54. Discover more in 1 Samuel 21:9.]

117. MERAB

King Saul has two daughters. Merab is the oldest.

When David kills Goliath, the expectation among the troops is that the king will give his oldest daughter to that man in marriage. We don't know if the men merely assume the king will do this or if that was his pledge. Regardless, he doesn't.

Later, however, Saul offers Merab as a wife for David if he'll go to war to fight the king's battles for him. But this is a ruse. Saul expects David to die in the military conflict, saving the king the trouble of killing David himself. Saul never suspects David will return victorious, but when he does, the king reneges on his promise and marries off Merab to another man, Adriel.

Saul never intended for David to marry Merab. Instead, the king uses his daughter to entice David to do something life-threatening. In this we see a father who exploits his daughter as bait to try to bring about his enemy's death.

Merab and Adriel have five sons. This is the last we hear about her. The story, however, is not over, for David has eyes for Merab's younger sister, Michal.

When have we ever made a promise we had no intention of keeping? When have we used someone else to accomplish our goals?

[Read about Merab in 1 Samuel 18:17–19. Discover more in 1 Samuel 17:25.]

118. MICHAL

King Saul's younger daughter is Michal. She loves David.

David plays a critical role in the success of King Saul and the nation of Israel. The king should be grateful, yet Saul's attitude toward David vacillates, with Saul often wanting to kill David out of jealousy.

When Saul learns that Michal loves David, the king hatches a plan to use her to bring about David's downfall. For a dowry, Saul requests proof that David has killed one hundred Philistines. Saul assumes David will die trying. Instead, David succeeds and presents evidence he's killed twice as many.

David and Michal marry.

When Michal learns of her father's latest plan to kill David, she helps her husband escape and covers for him. But when her father confronts her, she lies and says that David forced her to help him get away.

Later, when David flees for his life, Saul gives Michal to another man. Eventually, David arranges for Michal's return.

After David ascends to power, he brings the ark of the Lord back, celebrating wildly in praise to God. Michal criticizes his excessive public display of worship and despises him for his actions. Though she once loved him, she no longer does.

We can only guess why. Did his passionate celebratory dance repel her? Perhaps she gave her heart to her second husband. Or maybe it was because David married other women.

Regardless, Michal never has any children. Might David have rejected her because of her disapproval of his exuberant dance? Or maybe God punished her for criticizing David's passionate worship.

In any regard, her critical spirit is not attractive. Having a critical spirit never is.

When have we had a critical spirit? What should we do about it?

[Read about Michal in 1 Samuel 18:20–29 and 2 Samuel 6:16–23. Discover more in 1 Samuel 19:11–17 and 1 Samuel 25:44.]

119. AHIMELEK (1)

himelek is a priest. He lives in Nob. One of the times when David flees for his life from King Saul, he goes to the priest in Nob.

David's unexpected arrival troubles Ahimelek. But David lies. He assures the priest everything is okay, that he's on an urgent mission for the king.

David asks Ahimelek for food and a weapon. The only food Ahimelek has is some of the consecrated bread. He gives it to David. The only weapon Ahimelek has is Goliath's sword. He gives that to David too. Then David leaves.

When Saul learns that Ahimelek helped David escape, he orders the priest's execution. While none of his men are willing to kill a priest, Doeg the Edomite has no such reluctance.

Doeg kills Ahimelek, along with all the other priests from Nob.

Only Abiathar, Ahimelek's son, escapes. He flees and joins David. When David learns what happened, he realizes he's responsible for the death of the priests.

When is lying justified? When have we suffered for doing what we thought was right?

[Read about Ahimelek in 1 Samuel 21:1–9 and 1 Samuel 22:9–23. Discover more in Psalm 52.]

120. DOEG

Doeg the Edomite appears in only one passage in Scripture. His story intertwines with Ahimelek's.

When King Saul orders the execution of Ahimelek for assisting in David's escape, none of the king's men are willing to kill the priest. They are wise to respect the function of the priesthood, and they likely realize he is innocent of what the king is accusing him of. We applaud them for doing the right thing.

Yet there is one man, a foreigner, who has no such respect for the priesthood or for what is right. He is Doeg, from Edom.

When King Saul turns to Doeg and tells him to kill Ahimelek and all the other priests, he doesn't hesitate. That day, Doeg kills eighty-five priests.

But he doesn't stop his killing spree after obeying the king's command. He takes it upon himself to travel to the city of Nob. There he kills everyone and everything in the town. This includes all the men, women, and children, along with its cattle, donkeys, and sheep. He leaves nothing alive.

Doeg is an evil man who has no respect for the priesthood and no qualm about taking a life.

When told to do something wrong, do we resist like the king's men or comply like Doeg? How well do we do at respecting our spiritual leaders and thinking the best of them?

[Read about Doeg in 1 Samuel 22:9–23. Discover more in Proverbs 6:16–19.]

121. ABIGAIL (2)

In the time after Samuel anoints David, but before Bathsheba, David's on the run, hiding from the murderous intent of King Saul. It's at this point that David encounters Abigail.

Abigail is an intelligent, beautiful woman. Her husband, Nabal, lacks these traits. He's surly and mean. His servants call him wicked and say he listens to no one. Abigail agrees. She confirms his name means *fool* and says that folly follows him. Despite this, Nabal is also wealthy, with thousands of goats and sheep.

David and his men decide to protect Nabal's herdsmen and flocks, anticipating he will appreciate their efforts and one day reward them. But Nabal disrespects David's emissaries when they ask for food; he sends them away empty-handed. Boiling with anger, David plans to retaliate. He intends to kill Nabal and his men.

When the astute Abigail hears what happened, she acts without delay. She prepares food for David and his men. She meets his advancing army of four hundred. She humbles herself before him, assumes responsibility (while professing her innocence), wins David over, and stops the massacre.

Abigail confirms that she believes God will provide David with a lasting dynasty. She asks him to remember her when God gives him success. David accepts her words and her provisions. He blesses her.

Nabal roils with anger when he learns what his wife did. He has a stroke and later dies. David receives this news with glee, seeing it as God's vengeance on his behalf. David sends for Abigail so he can marry her. This may be David fulfilling her request when they first met or an honorable act to provide for her.

This takes place while David is on the run, so her new lifestyle is not an easy one. At one point, Abigail is captured, along with the rest of the families of David's men, but he rescues her. She and David have at least one son: Kileab (also called Daniel).

What we best remember about Abigail, however, is the bold action she took to avoid a massacre.

What bold step does God want us to take? How can our actions and our words bring about peace and prevent discord?

[Read about Abigail in 1 Samuel 25. Discover more in 2 Samuel 3:3 and 1 Chronicles 3:1.]

122. ABNER

A bner is the commander of King Saul's army. He's also Saul's first cousin. Abner serves Saul well.

After the king's death, Abner transfers his alliance to Saul's son Ish-Bosheth, making him king over all Israel in his father's place, with David ruling over Judah.

A battle rages between Israel (led by Abner) and Judah (led by Joab). During the confrontation, Joab's brother Asahel pursues Abner with determination. Abner calls back to Asahel and tells him to chase someone else instead. Asahel refuses and continues to hound Abner. Frustrated, Abner stops fleeing and thrusts the butt of his spear into Asahel's stomach, impaling him. He dies instantly.

With Joab's army pursuing Abner's, Abner calls for an end to the fighting to avoid further bloodshed. Joab agrees and commands his army to withdraw.

Later, King Ish-Bosheth accuses Abner of sleeping with his father's concubine. The text doesn't say if the charge is true or not, so we don't know if Abner is innocent or guilty.

Regardless, the allegation incenses Abner. Knowing that David is the rightful king, Abner defects to David's camp, promising to help David secure his rule over all of Israel instead of just Judah.

They have a feast, and David sends Abner away in peace to accomplish his plan.

But when Joab hears what David did, he's furious. He secretly sends for Abner. When Abner returns, Joab approaches him as if to give him a special message. Instead, Joab stabs Abner in the stomach and he dies. In doing so, Joab murders Abner to avenge Asahel's death.

How do we respond when we're accused of something? What do we think about taking revenge?

[Read about Abner in 2 Samuel 2:8–31 and 2 Samuel 3:6–37. Discover more in 2 Samuel 4:1.]

123. ISH-BOSHETH

Ish-Bosheth is the son of King Saul. After his father's death—
with the help of Abner, commander of Saul's army—Ish-
Bosheth assumes his father's throne. He reigns for two years.
There's little remarkable about him or his rule.

One story we have is when he confronts Abner for sleeping with
his father's concubine. Though we don't know if this is a legitimate
accusation or baseless, Abner reacts negatively and defects to
David's side. As part of their negotiations, David asks for his wife
Michal to be restored to him, even though her father—King Saul—
gave her in marriage to another man.

Michal, incidentally, is Ish-Bosheth's sister. He has no qualms
taking her from her current husband and giving her back to David.
We can only guess if Ish-Bosheth does this because he has no regard
for his sister or because he fears Abner and David. Nonetheless,
Michal is restored to David, whether she wishes it or not.

Abner's alliance with David, however, doesn't last long, for Joab
murders the commander during a time of peace, in an act of
revenge.

Likely unaware that Abner defected, Ish-Bosheth loses his
courage when he learns his army's commander is dead. Abner

brought the king into power. Without the commander to protect him, two of Ish-Bosheth's military leaders assassinate him.

Not only does Ish-Bosheth's life and reign end, so does the short rule of King Saul's descendants.

When have we falsely accused someone? When have we failed to defend our family for fear of what others might do?

[Read about Ish-Bosheth in 2 Samuel 2:8–11and 2 Samuel 3:6–15. Discover more in 2 Samuel 4.]

124. JOAB

Joab serves as the commander of David's army. He realizes much success as a military leader, but he has some severe character issues. Here are three stories about Joab.

As we learned in the chapter about Abner, after he defects to David's camp with a plan to bring all of Israel under David's rule, Joab—unbeknownst to David—summons Abner back and stabs him to death. He does this in retaliation for Abner killing his brother in battle. Joab, however, does this during a time of peace. This makes Abner's death a murder.

Next, during Absalom's coup to seize his father's throne, David runs for his life. Even so, he tells all his men to be gentle with Absalom when they encounter him. Everyone hears David's instruction, but Joab ignores it. He kills Absalom the first chance he gets. He doesn't care that he violates the king's command.

What we don't know, however, is if Joab does this because he thinks it's in David's best interest or because Absalom chose Amasa to lead his coup and didn't tap Joab. Regardless, Absalom is dead, and David is despondent over what Joab did.

In our third story of Joab, David makes Amasa—Joab's cousin —commander for life over his army instead of Joab. This may be to express his displeasure over Joab killing Absalom contrary to David's command. Regardless of David's motivation, Joab murders Amasa during a time of peace.

Though Joab did do some good in his life, we remember him for murdering Abner and Amasa, as well as killing Absalom.

What are we known for? How can we elevate the importance of our character over our achievements?

[Read about Joab in 2 Samuel 3:26–27, 2 Samuel 18:9–17, and 2 Samuel 20:9–10. Discover more in 1 Kings 2:5–6.]

125. BATHSHEBA

Bathsheba is a beautiful woman. Her husband, Uriah, is off fighting in David's army, while the king stays home in the comfort of his royal residence.

From the vantage of his palace rooftop, David sees Bathsheba bathing. He wants her.

Both are at fault. Bathsheba should have been more discreet, and David shouldn't have been looking. David summons her and sleeps with her. He later confesses committing adultery with her. Since adultery is a consensual relationship, this shows she's a willing participant. Given that she bathed in plain view of David's palace rooftop, she may have even been the instigator.

For those who don't want to view Bathsheba as an adulteress, a willing participant in an affair, the other perspective is that she's a victim. In this viewpoint, her rooftop bathing is an innocent act. When David sends for her, she feels powerless to decline the request of a sovereign king and lets him do to her what he wants. It's a sexual assault, a rape. Yet, David doesn't confess to rape but to adultery.

Regardless, Bathsheba becomes pregnant.

Attempting to cover up what happened, David calls Uriah back from the front lines and tries twice to send the soldier home. When that fails, David develops a battle plan that results in Uriah's death. Bathsheba mourns her husband's passing. Then David marries her.

Later, the prophet Nathan confronts David for his actions. Once exposed, David acknowledges his mistakes—adultery and murder—and seeks God. However, their child becomes sick and dies.

David and Bathsheba later have Solomon. Solomon eventually becomes king, just as David promised Bathsheba. Centuries later, Jesus is born. He is David and Bathsheba's direct descendant, through Solomon.

What steps should we take to protect us from having an affair? Are we doing all we can to lead a pure, God-honoring life?

[Read about Bathsheba in 2 Samuel 11–12. Discover more in 1 Kings 1:11–31.]

126. URIAH (1)

Despite being a foreigner, Uriah the Hittite is loyal to the nation of Israel, to King David, and to God. He's an honorable man, serving in the nation's army.

David stays home while his troops, including Uriah, are off fighting. It's during this time that David sleeps with Uriah's wife, Bathsheba, and she gets pregnant.

To cover up their coupling, David calls Uriah back from the front lines. After two failed attempts to send Uriah home to the arms of his wife, David resorts to plan B. He develops a battle strategy to bring about Uriah's death. Uriah unwittingly carries the plan with him when he returns to the front lines.

The commander implements David's strategy, and Uriah dies.

Uriah is a victim of events outside of his control. He did nothing wrong. Yet he's effectively executed anyway, all because of the king's affair and attempted cover-up.

Though we may view Uriah's life as a tragedy, we should remember him as a devout man of integrity and valor. This is his legacy.

And there's one more thing. Though not an ancestor of Jesus,

Uriah's name, nonetheless, appears in Matthew's genealogy of Jesus, whereas his wife's name is absent.

In this way, Scripture honors the admirable Uriah.

When we do what is right, do we expect everything to work out? Will we maintain our trust in God if we suffer unjustly?

[Read about Uriah in 2 Samuel 11. Discover more in Matthew 1:1–6.]

127. MEPHIBOSHETH

You may remember David's best friend, Jonathan, King Saul's son. Though Saul and all his sons, including Jonathan, die in battle, this doesn't mean his line is wiped out. Saul's grandson, Jonathan's son Mephibosheth, is still alive. The one physical characteristic we know about him is he is lame in both legs due to an accident when he was young.

As a sovereign king, David has the power to kill all members of the former king's family. This would ensure that no heir of the former king remained to try to reclaim the kingdom and overthrow the new ruler.

But King David doesn't follow this practice. In fact, he does the opposite. He seeks out members of Saul's family, not to end their life, but to demonstrate kindness. When he learns of Mephibosheth, he sends for the man.

It's easy to imagine Mephibosheth receiving this summons, no doubt expecting to be executed. He comes before David and bows down in honor. Though this would be the response of anyone called to appear before the king, I suspect Mephibosheth prostrates himself lower, longer, and more reverently than most. He must have assumed this was his last chance at survival and his final act in life.

Instead of ordering Mephibosheth's death, however, David elevates his best friend's son, granting him all his grandfather Saul's land and possessions. David also gives Mephibosheth a place of honor by giving him a permanent seat at the king's table.

David does all this without knowing much about Mephibosheth. The fact that he is Jonathan's son is all David needs to know.

In response to David's generosity, Mephibosheth remains appreciative and loyal to David throughout his life. Mephibosheth continues his commitment to the king even when his servant Ziba lies about him, slanders his reputation, and betrays him.

In all this we see Mephibosheth as an upright man.

What accepted practices should we stop doing to offer a God-honoring alternative? Is there a person we can show kindness to?

[Read about Mephibosheth in 2 Samuel 4:4, 2 Samuel 9:3–13, and 2 Samuel 19:24–30. Discover more about Ziba in 2 Samuel 16:1–4.]

128. NATHAN (2)

Nathan is a prophet during the reign of King David. The Bible has two stories about Nathan.

When David has established his kingdom and enjoys a time of peace, he shares an idea with Nathan. He wants to build a temple for the Lord.

Nathan tells David to proceed, that God is with him.

We don't know if Nathan gave David his blessing on his own accord or if it came from God. Nevertheless, that night God speaks to Nathan, telling him that David is *not* the one to build the temple. That privilege will fall to another.

In reading God's revelation to Nathan, it first seems as though it's a forward-looking prophecy to Jesus, who will establish a spiritual temple, one without end. Yet as we continue to read God's words, they shift into talking about a literal king who will accomplish this task.

Perhaps the prophecy refers to both Jesus and his eternal supernatural temple, as well as David's son Solomon and the physical temple he will build here on earth.

Regardless, David does not build a temple for God as he wished.

Another time Nathan confronts David by sharing a parable. It's of a rich man who steals his poor neighbor's sheep to feed guests. David is irate over the rich man's greed.

That's when Nathan reveals that David is the man in the story. Though he didn't take his neighbor's sheep, he did kill his neighbor after taking the man's wife. It's the story of David committing adultery with Bathsheba and killing her husband, Uriah, so the king can take her as his wife.

David confesses his sin. And though God forgives him, David suffers the consequences of his mistake for the rest of his life.

When have we approved of something only to have God later correct our perspective? How do we react when confronted with our sin?

[Read about Nathan in 2 Samuel 7:1–17 and 2 Samuel 12:1–25. Discover more in 1 Kings 1:7–46.]

129. TAMAR (2)

The story of Tamar is tragic. She's the beautiful daughter of King David and catches the eye of her half-brother, Amnon, who lusts for her. At the advice of his cousin, Amnon feigns illness and manipulates Tamar into his bedroom, duping David into innocently arranging the whole thing.

Once alone, Amnon grabs Tamar and solicits her. She refuses—three times. When her pleading fails to dissuade him, she talks about the implications: her disgrace and him appearing foolish and wicked. She even suggests they ask Dad for permission to marry.

Amnon won't listen. Lust drives him. He loses control and rapes her.

After this, his supposed love turns into an even more intense hate. He commands her to leave, but Tamar refuses. She says that rejecting her would be an even greater insult. Amnon has her forcibly removed from his presence.

Tamar, a victim of rape, lives in desolation with her brother Absalom.

What can we do to help the victims in our world? Who is one person we can help today?

[Read about Tamar in 2 Samuel 13:1–22. Discover more in 2 Samuel 13:23–33.]

130. AMNON (1)

Amnon is the oldest son of David. As the firstborn, we'd expect him to one day replace his father as king. Yet this is not to be. Though it may have been David's intent to make Amnon king, the young man's behavior and the consequences of what he did make it impossible.

The Bible tells us that Amnon falls in love with his half-sister Tamar. Yet the law of Moses prohibits them from having a physical relationship. Amnon doesn't care. He's obsessed. Lust overtakes him. He rapes his sister and then throws her from his bedroom as though she's disposable.

Tamar goes to live with her brother Absalom, who takes care of her. He also looks for a way to avenge her disgrace.

Three years later, he does. He has his men kill Amnon.

Though death is a disproportionate penalty for rape, Amnon deserves punishment. In his uncontrolled lust, he ruined his sister's life, robbing her of the potential her future held. His lack of restraint also brought about his death, which precluded him the opportunity to ascend to the throne in place of his father.

Just as one moment ruined his sister's life, it also resulted in a premature end to his.

What lessons can we learn from what Amnon did? What lessons can we learn from Absalom's reaction?

[Read about Amnon in 2 Samuel 13:1–39. Discover more in 2 Samuel 3:2–3.]

131. ABSALOM

Absalom is David's third son. Absalom's beautiful sister, Tamar, is raped by their conniving half-brother Amnon. Absalom comforts Tamar and avenges her dishonor by killing Amnon.

Though parents aren't responsible for what their children do, these events suggest David is a hands-off dad who may not have raised his children well or instilled in them a sense of right and wrong. We get implicit confirmation of this when the Bible says David never rebuked another son, Adonijah. It's likely David didn't attempt to correct Absalom or Amnon either.

This may be why Amnon takes advantage of his sister and Absalom takes revenge on Amnon. Rape and murder are not God's way to live. We know this, but Amnon and Absalom don't. Or might they think that as the king's sons they're above the law?

This attitude of doing whatever he wants carries forward in Absalom's life. He wants to become king. With his older brother Amnon out of the way, Absalom now has one less roadblock to achieve his goal.

Absalom doesn't even wait for his father to die. He orchestrates a coup to usurp his father's throne and seize control.

David and his entourage flee for their lives. When Absalom's rebellion falters and David reinserts himself as king, he tells his army to be gentle with his undeserving son. However, Joab, the commander of the army, disregards David's instructions and kills Absalom. This puts an end to Absalom's threat, as well as his sinful behavior.

Have we ever been like Absalom and tried to seize something that wasn't ours? Are we willing to show mercy to a family member or friend who did us wrong?

[Read about Absalom throughout 2 Samuel 13–18. Discover David's psalm when he fled from Absalom in Psalm 3.]

132 TAMAR (3)

Tamar is the daughter of Absalom. She is most beautiful. That's all we know about her. We can assume Absalom named her after her Aunt Tamar, her father's sister whom her Uncle Amnon raped. This aunt was taken in by her dad, where she lived in desolation.

By sharing her aunt's name, Absalom's daughter Tamar is linked to the tragedy that befell her aunt. We're left to wonder if this defines her or impacts her life. Yet it must have some ramifications.

Like Tamar, our name may be in memory of someone else, which may or may not have positive implications.

Yet our name—what it means or who it's connected to—need not dictate our future. We can pursue our own path.

Regardless of what our life is now, it need not limit what we become.

How can we live our own life, regardless of the labels people give us? How can we overcome our circumstances to become all God wants us to be?

[Read about Tamar in 2 Samuel 14:27. Discover other beautiful women in Job 42:14–15 and Esther 2:7.]

133. ABIATHAR

When Doeg the Edomite, under the order of King Saul, kills Ahimelek and eighty-five other priests, only Ahimelek's son Abiathar escapes.

Abiathar flees to David, who offers him sanctuary. Abiathar takes the ephod with him. This likely refers to the ephod Moses made for the priests to wear (Exodus 28). Symbolically, this shows the priesthood going with Abiathar and in support of David.

The ephod serves as a tool to approach God to seek his guidance. When David wants to inquire of the Lord, he tells Abiathar to bring the ephod. Abiathar seeks the Lord's guidance as prescribed. And God tells David what to do.

Much later during Absalom's coup, Abiathar and Zadok, another priest, leave Jerusalem with King David, taking the ark with them. But David sends them back to the city with the ark. There they can gather information, which their sons can relay to David. They do as instructed. Soon David's reign is restored, thanks in part to Abiathar sending him inside information.

When another of David's sons, Adonijah, conducts his coup, Abiathar aligns with him in support, but Zadok does not. This is one of the few times the two priests do not operate in unison.

After David's death, with his son Solomon firmly on the throne, the new king punishes Abiathar for his disloyalty to David. Solomon removes Abiathar from the priesthood and banishes him to his fields in Anathoth.

Though Abiathar served David well for most of his life, he didn't finish strong. He made a mistake and received punishment for it. This is the last we hear of Abiathar.

When people are disloyal, how do we determine if we're to offer mercy or punishment? What must we do to finish strong?

[Read about Abiathar in 2 Samuel 15:24–36, 1 Kings 1:7–27, and 1 Kings 2:20–27. Discover more in 1 Samuel 23:6–12 and 1 Samuel 30:7–8.]

134. ABISHAI

bishai is the brother of Joab, commander of King David's army. Scripture tells us that Abishai is one of David's mighty warriors, a subcommander of his army, and credited with impressive military victories.

He's also zealous for David, perhaps too much so. Or maybe he has a thirst for killing and vengeance. Here are two stories that reveal his nature.

First, when David flees for his life from King Saul, he and Abishai sneak into Saul's camp undetected. With Saul asleep, Abishai sees this as an opportunity to kill David's enemy. He asks David for permission to run his spear through the king.

David won't allow it. He reprimands Abishai, noting that Saul is the Lord's anointed, and they shouldn't harm him. David has confidence God will deal with Saul in his own way and timing.

Though Saul is intent on killing David, David refuses to reciprocate.

Another time, during Absalom's coup attempt, David again runs for his life. A man named Shimei curses the king as he flees, pelting him with rocks. Shimei calls David a murderer and a scoundrel.

Just as before, Abishai wants to defend David, this time by

cutting off Shimei's head. Again, David rebuffs Abishai and defers to God's judgment.

Both times, David stops Abishai from being overzealous and killing another person.

Are we zealous to a fault? When has someone rebuffed us for our eagerness to act?

[Read about Abishai in 1 Samuel 26:6–11 and 2 Samuel 16:9–13. Discover more in 2 Samuel 3:30, 2 Samuel 23:18, and 1 Chronicles 18:12.]

135. HUSHAI

Hushai is an Arkite. The Bible tells us little about the Arkites, other than that they descend from Noah's grandson Canaan. This makes Hushai a foreigner in Israel, a non-Jew. Yet he is also loyal to King David, serving as his confidant.

When Absalom attempts a coup against David, the king flees for his life. Hushai aligns with David and intends to leave with him. Yet David has a different idea. He sends Hushai back to advise Absalom, with the plan to give poor advice and thwart the recommendations of Absalom's other adviser, Ahithophel.

Though this is at significant personal risk should Absalom learn of his covert activities, Hushai does as David requests. Not only does Hushai successfully thwart the advice given to Absalom by Ahithophel, but he also sends reports back to King David about Absalom's plans.

As a result of Hushai's bold actions, David escapes Absalom's grasp and later reclaims his throne.

How loyal are we to our leaders? How willing are we to take a personal risk to do something daring?

[Read about Hushai in 2 Samuel 17:5–16. Discover more in 2 Samuel 15:32–37 and 1 Chronicles 27:33.]

136. AHITHOPHEL

Ahithophel is King David's counselor. Yet when Absalom attempts his coup against his father, Ahithophel shows no sign of loyalty to David and aligns himself with Absalom.

Ahithophel gives Absalom advice, which we later find out is correct. But Hushai—working under David's direction to foil Ahithophel—provides a conflicting recommendation, albeit for David's benefit and not Absalom's. Absalom accepts Hushai's counsel and rejects Ahithophel's.

When Ahithophel realizes Absalom ignored his advice, he goes home in disgrace. Once there, he puts his estate in order and hangs himself.

How do we react when we encounter an enormous embarrassment? What other options might Ahithophel have pursued?

[Read about Ahithophel in 2 Samuel 17:1–23. Discover more in 2 Samuel 15:31–36 and 2 Samuel 16:15–23.]

137. AMASA (1)

In Absalom's brief coup attempt against his father, he appoints Amasa as commander of his rebel troops. Amasa is the first cousin of Joab, who commands David's army.

During the rebellion, Joab kills Absalom. This occurs despite David's explicit command to spare his son's life. Though doing so ends the coup and restores David to power, David mourns his son's death and is angry with Joab.

David replaces Joab as commander of his army with Amasa, giving him a lifetime appointment. This is despite Amasa aligning with Absalom and helping facilitate his rebellion.

Unfortunately, Amasa's appointment doesn't last long. Joab murders him shortly after David promotes him.

This occurs when Joab approaches Amasa. Feigning friendship and even calling him brother, Joab plunges a dagger into the unsuspecting man's stomach. Amasa dies.

What can we learn from David promoting Amasa despite being part of Absalom's coup? How can we guard against people who act friendly toward us but will do us harm?

[Read about Amasa in 2 Samuel 17:25, 2 Samuel 19:13, and 2 Samuel 20:4–13. Discover more in 1 Kings 2:1–6.]

138. SOLOMON

After David and Bathsheba's first son dies, the pair later has Solomon. Solomon succeeds his father David as king, though an earlier coup—thankfully unsuccessful—by Absalom nearly kept this from happening. Another brother, Adonijah, also attempts to steal the throne before David makes Solomon king.

As David's successor, Solomon builds the temple his father yearned to construct. Solomon rules well, enjoys peace, and has a reputation for being wise, wiser than anyone else.

Yet for all his wisdom, Solomon makes an unwise decision. It's an action he repeats hundreds of times. He marries foreign women, something the Law of Moses forbids (Deuteronomy 7:3–4). In total, Solomon amasses seven hundred wives and three hundred concubines.

In his old age, his foreign wives turn his attention from the God his father served to the gods they serve. Solomon's heart is divided in loyalty between the one true God and the gods his wives worship.

Though Solomon received a great start in life and ruled with wisdom, his foreign wives distracted him from living a life fully devoted to the Lord, as his father, David, had done. This is a sad ending to an otherwise successful life.

What relationships do we have that may turn our focus away from God? Do we follow all of God's commands or assume, like Solomon, that some don't apply to us?

[Read about Solomon in 1 Kings 1–11. Discover more in 2 Samuel 12:24 and Nehemiah 13:26.]

139. ABISHAG

Abishag is a young, beautiful Shunammite woman. She's carefully selected to attend to King David in his old age. Despite her sleeping next to him to keep him warm, their relationship isn't sexual—though I'm sure people thought otherwise.

When the king dies, we might assume her ordeal is over. But it's not. After David's death, his son Adonijah requests, through Bathsheba, that her son Solomon, the new king, allow him to marry Abishag.

Though this seems like a reasonable request, Solomon sees this as Adonijah's attempt to elevate his standing in the kingdom and vie for leadership. His perceived power struggle is a threat to Solomon's reign. So Solomon executes Adonijah.

Abishag has her life in front of her, full of expectation, when she's tapped to serve the king. Then another man tries to use her to usurp his half-brother's throne. His ploy results in his execution.

We don't know what happens to Abishag after this.

How do we react when someone uses us? How should we respond to things outside our control?

[Read about Abishag in 1 Kings 1:1–4. Discover more in 1 Kings 2:13–25.]

140. ADONIJAH (1)

David's first four sons are Amnon, Kileab, Absalom, and Adonijah. Each one has a different mother, making them all half-brothers. Absalom kills Amnon for raping their sister Tamar. Then Absalom dies in a coup attempt. The Bible only mentions Kileab once, so he likely does nothing noteworthy nor notorious.

As a result, Adonijah may think he's next in line to become king. He attempts to assume the throne, but David installs Solomon as king instead.

Fearing for his life, Adonijah begs Solomon not to kill him. Solomon offers mercy to his older half-brother, who's also the biggest threat to his rule. Solomon basically says that if Adonijah behaves himself he will live, but if he does evil, then he must die.

All is fine for Adonijah until he asks Solomon's permission to marry Abishag, their father's personal assistant.

Though we don't know Adonijah's motivation—be it for love or for power—Solomon sees his half-brother's request as a move toward taking control of the kingdom and replacing Solomon as king.

Solomon orders Adonijah's execution.

Is there ever a time when it's unwise to offer mercy? What should we use as a guideline in determining what to do?

[Read about Adonijah in 1 Kings 1:5–53 and 1 Kings 2:13–25. Discover more in 2 Samuel 3:1–5.]

141. SONS OF KORAH (2)

There are several men named Korah in the Bible. The one we know best is the Levite Korah who rebels against Moses and God. Because of the uprising he leads, God kills Korah and his family—and presumably his three sons.

Therefore, it's not likely this Korah's sons—that is, his descendants—who we read about in the book of Psalms. But if it's a different Korah, we know nothing about him.

Regardless, these "Sons of Korah" are listed in the preamble in eleven of the 150 psalms. These introductory phrases are part of the original text, unlike subheadings that were later added, as we see throughout the rest of the Bible.

Though the Sons of Korah may have written each song, an alternate interpretation is that they performed them.

To have their names attached to these eleven psalms suggests they're skilled at what they do and enjoy a following. Their praise of God is noteworthy and an example that can inspire us.

What are we known for? How can we better praise God?

[Read about the Sons of Korah in the preambles of Psalms 42, 44 through 49, 84, 85, 87, and 88. Discover more in the preambles of Psalms 3, 50, 72, 89, and 90.]

142. ZADOK (1)

Zadok and Abiathar serve David as priests. The two work together in support of him. During Absalom's coup attempt, they both side with David. The pair covertly work to send information about Absalom's short-lived reign back to David's camp through their sons.

This is not the case, however, when Adonijah tries to insert himself as his father's successor. Though Abiathar defects to align himself with Adonijah's fleeting rebellion, Zadok does not. Zadok remains loyal to King David, along with Nathan the prophet and Benaiah, son of Jehoiada.

David quells Adonijah's uprising by pronouncing Solomon as his official replacement and installing him as king. Solomon could have ordered Abiathar's execution for supporting his half-brother's rebellion, but he does not. Though Solomon notes that the priest deserves to die, the wise king allows him to live because of his earlier service to David.

Solomon does, however, remove Abiathar as priest and sends him home to live. The king replaces him with the loyal Zadok.

Zadok proves himself as a worthy priest, in part for supporting David and Solomon as God's appointed kings.

How supportive are we of our leaders? Will others celebrate our loyalty?

[Read about Zadok in 1 Kings 1:5–45 and 1 Kings 2:35. Discover more in 2 Samuel 15:24–36.]

143. QUEEN OF SHEBA

The queen of Sheba hears about the stunning reputation of King Solomon. She's skeptical and travels to meet him. The queen wants to see if there is any truth to the reports she's heard.

Presenting him with gifts, she talks with Solomon at length. The king answers her every question, able to fully explain all things to her. He impresses her. She's also astounded by what she sees.

The queen affirms his great wisdom and immense wealth, declaring that what she heard fails to communicate the fullness of all she saw and experienced. She is in awe.

Solomon loads her up with gifts, and she returns home.

The queen of Sheba had to see to believe.

Do we have the faith to believe without seeing? How far will we go to discover what is true?

[Read about the queen of Sheba in 1 Kings 10:1–13. Discover more in Luke 11:29–31.]

144. AGUR

We commonly think of King Solomon as the author of the book of Proverbs. While this is mostly true, it's not completely correct. Proverbs also contains wisdom from Agur (as well as Lemuel, whom we'll cover in a bit).

Agur is the son of Jakeh. Neither man, however, appears anywhere else in Scripture, so we know nothing more about them from the biblical account. Yet what Agur writes does reveal his practical insights.

Sandwiched between his opening praises to God and his ending plethora of wise insights, is a key consideration.

He asks God for two things.

First is that God will keep falsehood and lies at bay. We can see this as him wanting protection from the untruths of others, as well as to not spread them himself.

His second request is that God will give him neither poverty nor wealth. He merely asks for his daily bread.

Though this may seem like a strange petition, he explains his rationale.

He worries that if he is satiated, he may turn from God, feeling a smug self-satisfaction. His counter concern is that if he has too little, he may steal to provide for his needs.

He wants to avoid both extremes. So asking for his daily bread, neither less nor more, is his petition.

What can we learn from Agur's two requests? Should we share his concern about not having enough or alternately of having too much?

[Read about Agur in Proverbs 30. Discover more in Matthew 6:9–13.]

145. LEMUEL

Immediately after the proverbs of Agur, we have the proverbs of Lemuel. The Bible refers to him as King Lemuel. Yet his name doesn't appear elsewhere in Scripture, so we don't know what he's the king of.

Nor do we know anything else about him, aside from his wise sayings. Yet even this label misleads us. What follows this grand introduction are not the sayings of Lemuel, but instead the words of his mother.

In this brief passage of only nine verses, he merely preserves her words for us to read today, but we should be glad he did.

There are two primary thoughts in these proverbs from King Lemuel's mom.

First is a warning to stay away from wine and beer, lest they impair our memory. Beer is for the perishing, while wine is for those in anguish.

Second is the reminder to speak for those who cannot speak for themselves, to stand up for the destitute and judge fairly.

King Lemuel has a wise mother, and he is wise for recording her wisdom for us to read.

What have our parents taught us that we need to share with others? What can we pass on to the next generation?

[Read about Lemuel in Proverbs 31:1–9. Discover more in Proverbs 1:8–9.]

146. REHOBOAM

After King Solomon dies, his son Rehoboam succeeds him as king. Jeroboam opposes him.

Jeroboam, one of Solomon's officials, had received a prophetic word that he would become king over ten of the tribes of Israel, with Solomon's descendants ruling over the tribe of Judah.

Jeroboam, along with all of Israel, approach Rehoboam with a request. They ask him to lighten the people's load. If he does, they'll surely serve him.

Wisely, Rehoboam asks for three days to consider it.

The king seeks advice from the elders who had served Solomon during his reign. They think Jeroboam's request makes sense and recommend that Rehoboam agree to it.

But Rehoboam doesn't like their advice. He consults with his peers, young men he grew up with and who were now serving him as king. They give him the opposite counsel. This is what Rehoboam wants to hear.

Jeroboam and the people return in three days to learn Rehoboam's response. The king doesn't give them a favorable answer. He refuses to lighten their load. Instead, he'll do the opposite. He'll demand even more of them than his father.

The people reject Rehoboam as king and follow Jeroboam. Rehoboam is left with only the tribe of Judah to rule over, just as the prophet predicted.

Who should we get advice from? What do we do when we receive counsel we don't like?

[Read about Rehoboam in 1 Kings 12:1–24. Discover more in 1 Kings 14:21–31 and Matthew 1:7.]

147. ASA

Asa is the king of Judah. He's the son of Abijah, the son of Rehoboam, the son of Solomon, the son of David. This means Asa is King David's great-great-grandson.

He reigns for forty-one years. Scripture says he does what is right in God's eyes. And he remains fully committed to the Lord throughout his life. This is the opposite of his father, Abijah, who served as an evil king.

Asa rids the land of idol worship and deposes his grandmother Maakah from her position as queen mother for her worship of Asherah. He brings about much needed spiritual reform to the nation of Judah during his rule.

Even so, his reign as king is marked by a continual war against Israel. This shows us that doing what is right and honoring God doesn't guarantee a life absent of conflict.

There's one more thing we can affirm Asa for. He raises his son, Jehoshaphat, well. Like his father, Jehoshaphat does what is right and follows the Lord. This is unlike so many of the other kings of Judah who do not prepare their sons to rule in a God- honoring way.

We applaud Asa for serving God as he leads the people of Judah and for raising his son to do the same.

When we do what is right, do we expect God to bless us with a comfortable life? What are we doing to prepare the next generation to serve the Lord?

[Read about Asa in 1 Kings 15:8–24 and 1 Kings 22:41–44. Discover more in Matthew 1:8.]

148. AHAB (1)

After Solomon's reign, the nation of Israel splits into two countries. David's line continues to rule the nation of Judah, while other kings reign over the rest of Israel. Both nations have God as their legacy, but the kings of Israel are consistent in not following him. They rebel and do evil.

One such king, who reigns about a century after David, is Ahab. He's the evilest king of Israel so far. He establishes the worship of foreign gods, Asherah and Baal, instead of God.

He marries Jezebel, a woman even more wicked than himself. Though we can criticize her for her negative influence on her husband, he alone is at fault for what he does.

Ahab begins his twenty-two-year rule as king of Israel while Asa, a good king, reigns in Judah. When Asa dies, his son Jehoshaphat succeeds him. Jehoshaphat is also a God-honoring king like his father.

Though Ahab and Jehoshaphat are opposite from a faith perspective, their nations have a common heritage and a common enemy, the nation of Aram. When Ahab asks Jehoshaphat to join forces in battle to retake the town of Ramoth Gilead, Jehoshaphat agrees.

But he also wants to seek God's counsel. Ahab's four hundred prophets all predict victory. Jehoshaphat, however, wants input from the Lord's prophets. Ahab knows of one, Micaiah. But the king doesn't like him because the prophet never predicts anything good.

After first sarcastically agreeing with the other four hundred prophets, Micaiah then speaks God's truth. He says Israel will face defeat if they go to battle, and he says Ahab will not return, implying he will die in the skirmish.

Attempting to avoid this, Ahab disguises himself as a chariot soldier so that he won't stand out as a target. But a random arrow hits him, and he dies.

Is there ever a time when we should align ourselves with someone who is evil and doesn't share our faith? When we seek counsel, do we believe the majority opinion or follow the single voice who represents God?

[Read about Ahab throughout 1 Kings 16–22. Discover more in Micah 6:16.]

149. OBADIAH (4)

O badiah is a devout believer of God. (He is not the prophet Obadiah, who lives much later.) The Bible contains only one story about this Obadiah, who serves as palace administrator for the evil King Ahab.

During the time of Ahab, king of Israel, there's a three-year drought, which produces a famine. This is as the prophet Elijah proclaimed.

King Ahab's wife, Jezebel, strives to kill all the prophets of God. Yet Obadiah protects one hundred of them, hiding them in two caves. And despite there being a drought and famine, he also supplies them with food and water. He does this at great personal risk, for if Queen Jezebel finds out what he's doing, she'll surely kill him.

In the middle of this, Ahab dispatches Obadiah to search for springs of water and grass to feed his horses and mules.

As Obadiah goes about his assignment, he meets Elijah. Obadiah bows before the prophet.

Then Obadiah asks a curious question: "What have I done wrong?"

For the past three years, King Ahab has been conducting an

unsuccessful manhunt for Elijah. Obadiah fears that when he reports Elijah's whereabouts to the king, God's Spirit will whisk the prophet away to another place. Obadiah worries the king will kill him in frustration for giving a false report.

Elijah promises he won't disappear. He pledges he'll come before King Ahab that very day.

Obadiah tells Ahab where Elijah is, and the king goes out to meet him. A huge showdown is about to take place between Elijah and the prophets of Baal.

What great personal risk are we willing to take to serve God? What lessons can we learn from Obadiah?

[Read about Obadiah in 1 Kings 18:1–16. Discover more in 1 Kings 17:1 and 1 Kings 18:17–40.]

150. JEZEBEL (1)

Ahab, Israel's evilest king so far, marries Jezebel, the daughter of a foreign ruler. Under her influence, Ahab worships her gods instead of the true God. Jezebel also hunts down and kills God's prophets, while providing sanctuary for hundreds of the prophets of Baal and Asherah.

God's prophet Elijah has a public confrontation with the prophets of Baal and Asherah. God and Elijah win, and Elijah kills all the prophets of Baal and Asherah who are present.

In retaliation, Jezebel threatens to kill Elijah. While he's on the run, the queen adds to her crimes. Here's what happens:

Ahab wants a specific vineyard from Naboth because it's near the palace. But Naboth refuses to sell it to Ahab or trade with him. This infuriates the king, but it's Jezebel who acts to get the vineyard for her husband.

She commands the city elders where Naboth lives to gather the people and pay two men to slander Naboth in front of witnesses. They're to testify that Naboth cursed God (as well as the king) a crime warranting execution.

The city leaders do as she instructed. Then the people stone Naboth to death. Ahab takes possession of the dead man's vineyard.

Eventually, Jezebel suffers a gruesome death. She's tossed from a balcony and stomped to death by horses. This is the price for her evil actions, just as prophesied.

Are we doing everything we can to promote the right worship of God and shun evil? When have we gone too far to do something for a family member or friend?

[Read about Jezebel in 1 Kings 21:5–23 and 2 Kings 9:7–37. Discover more in 1 Kings 18:4 and 19:1–2.]

151. JEHOSHAPHAT (3)

J ehoshaphat is the great-great-grandson of King Solomon. Though Solomon's father David ruled well as a man after God's own heart, Solomon's heart was divided and many succeeding kings in their family line did more evil than good.

Jehoshaphat is an exception.

Scripture calls him a good king, just like his father Asa. He follows his father's example and doesn't stray from how his dad raised him.

During Jehoshaphat's twenty-five-year reign, his country, Judah, experiences a time of peace with the nation of Israel. Although Jehoshaphat allies himself with Israel's evil king Ahab in conducting a joint military campaign, God doesn't criticize Jehoshaphat for doing so.

Overall, the Bible characterizes Jehoshaphat as someone who does what is right in God's eyes. Yet this doesn't mean he does everything he should have. No one does.

Despite ruling with wisdom and following God, Jehoshaphat fails to remove the high places where the people go to offer sacrifices and burn incense, contrary to God's command.

Though we could fault Jehoshaphat for this one failure,

remember that the Bible characterizes him as doing what is right. This is his legacy.

Do we judge others on what they do right or what they do wrong? As Asa did with Jehoshaphat, what are we doing to train the next generation to follow God?

[Read about Jehoshaphat in 1 Kings 22. Discover more in Matthew 1:1–8.]

152. ELIJAH (2)

Our first encounter with Elijah in Scripture occurs when he goes to King Ahab to warn of a famine-producing drought; no dew or rain will fall until Elijah says so. During this famine, God provides for Elijah, first through ravens at a brook and later through a widow in Zarephath.

After three years of no rain, God sends Elijah back to Ahab. Elijah challenges Ahab's prophets of Baal and Asherah to a spiritual competition of sorts. Elijah and the prophets will each build an altar and pray for fire to rain down from the sky and ignite the offering. The deity who answers will prove he is God.

The 450 prophets of Baal and four hundred prophets of Asherah build their altar and cry out to their gods to send fire. Nothing happens.

Elijah taunts them.

They plead even more, dancing with fervor and mutilating themselves to get their gods' attention. Still, nothing happens.

Now it's Elijah's turn. He builds his altar and arranges the sacrifice on it. Then he drenches everything with water. He prays a simple prayer to God—no pleading, dancing, or self-affliction—

asking the Almighty to send fire so the people will know he is the one true God.

Fire shoots down from the sky, burning up the sacrifice, the wood, the stones, and the soil around the altar, even consuming the water Elijah poured on everything.

The people bow low in worship, proclaiming the Lord is God.

Instead of joining the celebration, however, Elijah instructs the people to seize the prophets of Baal and Asherah. He executes all 850 of them.

Elijah prays for rain and a downpour occurs.

This would be the perfect place to end our story, but there's more.

When evil Queen Jezebel learns what Elijah did, she threatens to kill him. He runs away in fear.

Yet God doesn't give up on his fickle prophet. He reveals his presence and speaks to Elijah in a quiet whisper. Among other things, God tells him to go and anoint Elisha to succeed him.

Elijah does, and later God takes him up into heaven in a whirlwind. *That's* the end of the story.

Do we have the courage to do what God says even when the odds are against us? Have we ever floundered under the threats of one person, like Elijah did?

[Read about Elijah in 1 Kings 17–19 and 2 Kings 1–2. Discover more in James 5:17–18.]

153. ELISHA

We earlier saw that Moses appointed Joshua to succeed him. Though preparing someone to carry on our ministry or lead our tribe when we're gone is a wise move, the Bible has too few examples of this occurring. Elijah and Elisha are a noteworthy exception. After Elijah anoints Elisha to succeed him as prophet, he mentors his protégé.

With Elisha trained to take over as God's prophet, both men know Elijah's time on earth is about to end. Elisha insists on staying with his mentor for as long as possible. Elijah asks his protégé if he has any final requests.

He does. He asks to inherit a double portion of Elijah's spirit.

"This is a most difficult request," Elijah says, "but if you see me as I am taken from you, God will provide what you've asked."

They continue walking. Suddenly, a chariot of fire, drawn by horses of fire, appears and separates the two men. Elisha watches Elijah ascend toward heaven in a whirlwind. And that's the last Elisha sees him.

Yet the fact that Elisha sees Elijah as he's taken confirms that God will grant Elisha a double portion of his mentor's spirit.

What a powerful way for him to begin his work for God.

Is there someone we can mentor to continue our ministry when we're gone? Do we live our life in such a way that someone would want to inherit a double portion of our spirit?

[Read about Elisha in 2 Kings 2–8 and 13:14–21. Discover another man who did not die in Genesis 5:24.]

154. NAAMAN (3)

Naaman is an accomplished military leader for the king of Aram. The Bible calls him a valiant soldier, but he suffers from a limiting physical ailment. He has leprosy. It's a contagious skin disease that can cause a loss of feeling, flesh decay, and even deformation. (You may recall that Miriam contracted leprosy later in her life.)

A band of raiders from Aram make incursions into Israel. They capture a young girl who's forced to work in the household of Naaman. Though she has every right to be bitter about her situation, she tells him of the prophet Elisha, who can heal him of his terrible disease.

Naaman seeks permission from his king to go to Elisha to receive healing. In anticipation of a successful outcome, Naaman prepares gifts to give to the prophet in gratitude. The king of Aram also drafts a letter for the king of Israel, telling *him* to heal Naaman of his leprosy.

The king of Israel is distraught when he reads the letter, knowing he can't heal Naaman, or anyone else, of leprosy. He rips his royal robes in distress, thinking this is an excuse for the king of Aram to pick a fight.

When Elisha hears what happened, he sends a message instructing the king of Israel to send Naaman to him. Yet when Naaman arrives, the prophet doesn't even bother to see him. Instead, Elisha sends a message to Naaman telling him to wash seven times in the Jordan River. This will restore his flesh and take away his leprosy.

Offended that Elisha won't even talk to him and insulted at the instruction to wash in the Jordan River instead of one of the preferable waterways back home, Naaman storms off in a huff. But his attendants encourage him to do exactly what Elisha's message directed.

He does and receives God's healing.

Naaman affirms the power of God and pledges to worship him.

Like Naaman, will we humble ourselves to receive what we want? Do we believe God can heal us today?

[Read about Naaman in 2 Kings 5. Discover more in Luke 4:27.]

155. GEHAZI

Gehazi is the servant of Elisha.

The first time we encounter Gehazi is in the story about the Shunammite woman. When her only son dies, she seeks Elisha. Elisha gives his staff to Gehazi and dispatches him. He instructs his servant to rush to the boy and lay the staff on his face.

Gehazi does as instructed, but the child doesn't come back to life.

When Elisha arrives at the woman's home, he raises the boy from the dead. He sends Gehazi to call the boy's mother. Elisha presents her with her son, now very much alive.

The second time we read about Gehazi is in the story of Elisha healing Naaman of leprosy. When Naaman does as Elisha instructed, his skin is restored, and the leprosy is gone.

Yet Elisha won't accept any of the gifts Naaman offers.

Thinking that Elisha is wrong to refuse Naaman's generosity, Gehazi runs after Naaman. He lies to the man, asking for money and clothes. Naaman gladly gives what he requested and more.

Gehazi receives the gifts and hides them in his house.

When Elisha confronts Gehazi, the servant denies any wrongdoing. Yet in his spirit, Elijah saw exactly what happened.

As punishment, Elisha curses Gehazi—and his descendants forever—with Naaman's leprosy. Gehazi's skin turns white with a leprous infection.

Though we don't know if Gehazi is to blame for not being able to raise the Shunammite woman's son from the dead, we do know he failed. And when he went against Elisha's wishes to get some of Naaman's gifts and then lied about it, he received punishment for his actions.

When have we reacted selfishly or out of greed? What consequences of our sins will affect future generations?

[Read about Gehazi in 2 Kings 4:11–37 and 2 Kings 5:19–27. Discover more in 2 Kings 8:1–5.]

156. JONAH (1)

Jonah is the best known of the Bible's so-called minor prophets. He runs away from God and spends three days in the belly of a large fish. There he has plenty of time to think about his disobedience to God.

When the fish spits him onto the shore, God speaks to Jonah again. "Go to Nineveh. Once you arrive, I'll give you a message for the people."

This time Jonah obeys, but he doesn't have a good attitude.

We don't know if Jonah says exactly what God tells him to or if he paraphrases it to fit his lack of interest. But what he says is both succinct and blunt. "In forty days, Nineveh will be destroyed."

He doesn't provide correction or offer a hopeful alternative. He states the outcome as fact, providing no instruction for the people to repent. We may wonder how much Jonah cares about the people he preaches to. Or if he even wants them to repent.

He doesn't.

We later learn that Jonah longs to see the destruction of Nineveh. This is because Nineveh is the capital (or principal city) of Assyria, a longtime enemy of Judah and Israel. Surely Jonah and all his people would have cheered to see Assyria fall. They would see this as God's vindication, rescuing them from their adversaries.

It's no wonder Jonah puts little effort into his message.

Despite this, the people of Nineveh believe God will do as Jonah said. They fast. They humble themselves in the hope God may relent and offer them compassion.

Forty days come and forty days go, with Nineveh avoiding the destruction God had planned.

Yet Jonah isn't pleased that the people of Nineveh responded to his message and lived. Instead, our story ends with him complaining to God about his grace. This is the last we hear of Jonah.

When God tells us to do something, do we obey or run away? When we obey God's instructions, do we have a good attitude?

[Read about Jonah in the book of Jonah. Discover more in Luke 11:29–32.]

157. ATHALIAH (2)

Athaliah is an evil woman. She encourages her son, the king, to make some ill-advised decisions. He does and is assassinated later. Upon his death, Athaliah seizes control and inserts herself as queen. Her lust for power consumes her, so much that she kills all the members of the royal family, including her own grandchildren.

One baby, however, escapes the queen's execution mandate. This child is Joash. His aunt Jehosheba risks her life to save him from premature death. Six years later, the priest—with the support of the Levites and heads of leading families—crowns Joash, the rightful heir to the throne, as king.

Athaliah flies into a rage. She accuses them of treason. To express her outrage, she rends her clothes. But she can't change what happened. At the direction of the priest, the army kills her.

The country celebrates her death and calm returns.

Athaliah could have positively influenced her son and helped him rule wisely. She could have protected and groomed his successor, one of her grandsons. Had she done so, the people might have celebrated her life. Instead, they cheered her death.

How might people remember us? Do we do things to help others, or do we only seek to elevate ourselves?

[Read about Athaliah in 2 Kings 11:1–16. Discover another evil queen in 1 Kings 21.]

158. JEHOSHEBA

Jehosheba is the daughter of King Jehoram and the sister of King Ahaziah, both kings of Judah. When Ahaziah is murdered, Jehosheba's mother, Athaliah, seizes the throne and proclaims herself as queen, ordering the execution of the royal family—her own family.

At great personal risk, Jehosheba takes bold action to keep her nephew Joash from being killed by his evil grandmother. Jehosheba has little time to consider her actions when she rescues Joash from among the royal princes who are about to be killed.

Jehosheba hides Joash and his nurse in the temple for six years.

When Joash is seven, he's crowned king and his power-hungry grandmother is slain. The people rejoice and peace returns, all because of the boy-king and his aunt who made it possible.

Jehosheba plays a decisive role in protecting the rightful heir to the throne, keeping him alive so that he can one day rule and restore calm to the land.

Sometimes we must react quickly, with only a moment to analyze the situation. May we all be like Jehosheba, who acted decisively to do the right thing without concern for her own well-being.

Apart from these two passages that tell of Jehosheba's great valor, the Bible doesn't mention her again. Though she may have lived in seclusion in the temple with her nephew and his nurse, it's quite possible she died along with the rest of her family. She might have sought to save herself first, but she placed a priority on saving her nephew instead, assuring that her brother's legitimate heir would one day rule in his place.

What's something we ought to do, regardless of the risk? Are we willing to face death so that someone else may live?

[Read about Jehosheba in 2 Kings 11:2 and 2 Chronicles 22:11. Discover another woman who saves a baby—her son—in Exodus 2:1–10.]

159. JOASH (7)

Young, orphaned Joash lives in the temple for six years, where his nurse cares for him. He's hiding from the queen, his murderous, power-hungry grandmother. The priest is Joash's uncle, Jehoiada, the husband of Jehosheba. We can envision the priest teaching and guiding his young nephew.

When Joash turns seven, Jehoiada anoints the boy as the rightful king of Judah and orders the death of the queen. Though this sounds like a coup, it serves to reestablish the rightful rule by putting the former king's son into power.

Under Jehoiada's influence, Joash rules well.

But after Jehoiada dies, Joash falters. This may be why officials in his court conspire against him and assassinate him. This is a sad legacy to his once-promising start. His son, Amaziah, succeeds him as king.

Though Joash's forty-year reign as king of Judah began well, he didn't finish well.

Are we willing to listen to those who advise us? Is there someone we can guide to make God-honoring decisions?

[Read about Joash in 2 Kings 11–12. Discover another boy who became king in 2 Kings 22:1–2.]

160. ZECHARIAH (1)

We find many men throughout Scripture named Zechariah. The Bible may have more Zechariahs in it than any other name. With many obscure mentions throughout the Bible—fifty-nine times in nine books—it's impossible to determine accurately how many there are, but there are perhaps as many as twenty-two men named Zechariah in Scripture.

The main three are Zechariah (1), the king of Israel; Zechariah (15), the prophet, and Zechariah (22), the father of John the Baptist.

Zechariah (1) is notable because he's the first one mentioned in Scripture. He is a king of Israel—and evil.

He is the son of Jeroboam II, the son of Jehoash, the son of Jehoahaz, the son of Jehu. They are all kings of Israel. We'll see shortly why this is significant.

Zechariah—like all the kings of Israel after the nation split in two—is a sinful king. He does evil in the Lord's eyes, as did his predecessors. His reign lasts only six months. Shallum assassinates him, then replaces him as king. Interestingly, Shallum's reign is even shorter, lasting just one month, when he is likewise assassinated.

Though some evil kings enjoyed a long reign, Zechariah does not.

Before Zechariah's great-great-grandfather—Jehu—becomes king, he kills all King Ahab's descendants, along with his chiefs, close friends, and priests. No one survives. Then Jehu kills all the prophets of Baal and destroys their temple.

Jehu's actions please God and accomplish all God intended to do to the house of the evil king Ahab. Therefore, God promises Jehu that his descendants will rule to the fourth generation.

Despite this promising start, however, Jehu fails to keep God's laws with his whole heart. He continues the sins of former kings.

Even so, God fulfills his promise to Jehu that his reign will continue for four generations. Zechariah is the fourth. They are all evil.

What might we enjoy—even though undeserved—because of something one of our ancestors did? What are we doing to build on our lives for future generations?

[Read about Zechariah in 2 Kings 15:8–12. Discover more in 2 Kings 10:1–35, 2 Kings 13:9, 2 Kings 14:16, and 2 Kings 14:29.]

161. JOSIAH (1)

J osiah is a child when he becomes king, a mere eight years old. He rules for thirty-one years and does right in God's eyes, just as his ancestor King David had done.

Eight years into his reign, which makes him sixteen, he seeks God, just like David. Four years later, he purges the nation of idol worship. In his eighteenth year as king, he sets about to purify the land and the temple.

He orders that the offerings given at the temple be used to repair it. While doing the renovations, the high priest finds the Book of the Law in the temple. While we don't know how long God's Word had been misplaced, its contents surprise Josiah and all the people as something they had no knowledge of.

Upon hearing its words, Josiah tears his clothes in agony to display his remorse over what prior generations had done in disobeying God and disrespecting his worship. He sends his aides to consult with the prophetess Huldah to seek the Lord over what to do.

She confirms that God will indeed enforce the punishment warned about in the book for the people's persistent rebellion against him. Yet because Josiah had humbled himself before God, the Lord promises that the king will not witness destruction during his lifetime. He will see peace.

The promised punishment will happen later. But it will happen —just as God had already done to the nation of Israel to punish them for their ongoing sins.

Then Josiah celebrates Passover like never before, something not seen during the time of the kings or even the time of the judges. It's an extravagant observance lasting seven days.

How do we expect God to respond when we humble ourselves before him? What can we do to celebrate God and worship him more fully?

[Read about Josiah in 2 Chronicles 34–35. Discover more in 1 Kings 13:2 and 2 Kings 22–23.]

162. AMOS (1)

Chronologically, Amos follows Jonah and slightly overlaps with Hosea. He's also a contemporary of Isaiah. Occupationally he works as a shepherd and doesn't think of himself as a prophet.

In fact, he confirms to the priest Amaziah that he isn't a prophet nor the son of a prophet. Yet God told him to prophesy, so he did. When God called him, he was tending a flock and caring for sycamore-fig trees.

Amos proclaims God's truth during the reigns of kings Uzziah of Judah and Jeroboam II of Israel. He foretells judgment on many nations, including Judah, but Israel receives his primary focus.

In general, his message to all the nations is that they have sinned, and God will punish them.

Through all this, Amos is faithful to God's call on his life and ministry.

Do we need credentials to serve God? When he calls us to do something, do we tell him we're not able or do we say yes?

[Read about Amos in Amos 1:1 and Amos 7:14–15. Discover a parallel story in Matthew 9:9.]

163. ISAIAH

Isaiah son of Amoz is a faithful and long-serving prophet whose ministry spans the reigns of four kings of Judah: Uzziah, Jotham, Ahaz, and Hezekiah.

Isaiah is the prophet who delivers God's messages to King Hezekiah. The first message promises deliverance from the advancing army. The second is a pair of announcements about Hezekiah's death, with the second one correcting the first.

Does this mean Isaiah got it wrong?

No. Isaiah accurately relays God's message to Hezekiah. But when Hezekiah humbly asks God for a reprieve, the Almighty changes his mind and gives Isaiah the update.

But Isaiah is better known for his amazing prophecies about the coming Savior, the Messiah, which may be why Isaiah is so beloved by followers of Jesus and the most popular of all the prophets in Scripture. This may be in part because he also wrote one of the most cherished of all passages about Jesus:

For to us a child is born, to us a son is given, and the government will be on his shoulders. And he will be called Wonderful Counselor, Mighty God, Everlasting Father, Prince of Peace. (Isaiah 9:6 NIV)

New Testament writers either refer to or quote this amazing verse four times, with it showing up in Matthew, Mark, Luke, and Acts. In total, the New Testament references or cites Isaiah's work seventy-nine times, far more than any other prophet. (Only the Psalms garner more New Testament connections, at eighty-one.)

Overall, Isaiah comes in fourth on the list of Old Testament people with the most mentions in the New Testament, coming in after Moses, Abraham, and David.

In addition to Isaiah being a faithful prophet of God with a long ministry, we can applaud him for his impact on the people of his day, the early church, and us now.

What are we doing to impact the people around us? What can we do to encourage future generations?

[Read about Isaiah in 2 Kings 19–20. Discover more in the book of Isaiah.]

164. HOSEA

God speaks to Hosea, son of Beeri. The Almighty calls the young man to be his prophet. In a shocking move, however, God tells Hosea to marry a prostitute.

God doesn't tell Hosea which prostitute to marry. Hosea gets to choose. We don't know his selection criteria, but he picks Gomer. They marry, but they don't have a happy life as husband and wife.

They have a son. Then Gomer has two more children, but the subtext suggests Hosea doubts he's their father.

God prompts Hosea to use his relationship with Gomer and her illegitimate offspring as sermon illustrations in his scathing rebuke against the nations of Israel and Judah for their unfaithfulness to God.

This may embarrass Gomer, or maybe she's bored. Regardless, she runs off and takes up with another lover.

Yet God tells Hosea to go after her and bring her home. Hosea finds Gomer. He must buy her back, that is, he redeems her. Then he tells her to stop running around, to be faithful to only him. In doing so he offers her undeserved love and even accepts her two kids who were likely fathered by other men.

Hosea married Gomer even though she was undeserving. And he offered her redeeming love when she ran away.

So it is with God and us.

How willing are we to obey God when he tells us to do something outrageous? What if it's something we don't want to do or is painful?

[Read about Hosea in Hosea 1–3. Discover more in Romans 9:25–26.]

165. GOMER (2)

Gomer is a prostitute. We can assume she offers her body to other men to ensure her survival: food, water, and clothes. Or perhaps she's merely promiscuous.

Either way, she isn't marriage material. Yet, God's prophet Hosea marries her anyway.

Gomer and Hosea have a son, Jezreel.

Then she has two more children, but Hosea questions if he is their father. One is a girl, Lo-Ruhamah. The other is a boy, Lo-Ammi.

After that, unfaithful Gomer abandons her husband and three children. She runs away and takes up with another lover.

Shockingly, Hosea goes after her. The prophet buys her freedom. He tells her to stop chasing other men, to return home, and to be faithful to him. He offers her a love she doesn't deserve.

Hosea married Gomer even though she didn't deserve it. Later he redeemed her after she left him for another man.

Hosea's astonishing actions toward the sinful Gomer hint at God's unconditional love for us. And Gomer's lifestyle reminds us that we are all sinful people, undeserving of Jesus redeeming us and becoming his pure, spotless bride.

How can we move beyond our past to accept God's unconditional love for us? How does knowing that God has already forgiven our sins help us to forgive ourselves?

[Read about Gomer in Hosea 1:2–8 and Hosea 3:1–3. Discover more in Romans 5:8.]

166. JEZREEL

Jezreel is the first son of Hosea and Gomer. His name is an allusion to a place called Jezreel. Though there are many people in the Bible who have a place named after them, this may be the first time in Scripture we see a person named after a place.

What happened in Jezreel is notorious. This is where the overzealous—or perhaps power-hungry—Jehu slays all who remain in the family of evil king Ahab. He also murders the king's advisors, close friends, and priests. Though God wants Ahab punished for his ungodly behavior, there's no hint this extends to his counselors, friends, and priests.

The arrival of Hosea's son foreshadows the impending arrival of God's punishment on the nation of Israel, ending their existence as a country. Though the stated reason for this judgment is Jehu's massacre, what he did represents the nation's repeated rejection of God over several centuries.

Jezreel's birth signals the end of the nation of Israel.

What does our name mean? How do we react to having that connection?

[Read about Jezreel in Hosea 1:4–5. Discover more in 2 Kings 10:11 and Hosea 2:21–23.]

167. LO-RUHAMAH

Lo-Ruhamah is the daughter of Gomer, likely the result of adultery. Her mom, a former prostitute, cheats on her husband, Hosea, and has an affair with someone more appealing.

As directed by God, Hosea names his wife's illegitimate child. He calls her Lo-Ruhamah, which means *no pity* or *not loved*. Yet we understand why he rejects Lo-Ruhamah, whom someone else fathered.

What a terrible label to have attached to you. What a condemning legacy to carry. Every time someone says her name, it serves as a painful reminder to Lo-Ruhamah of being rejected by the only man in her life.

Eventually Hosea reconciles with his wife and accepts Lo-Ruhamah as his daughter. At last, he offers her love.

We wonder how Lo-Ruhamah responds. Does she rise above the shameful circumstance of her conception, or does she remain forever wounded by what her mother did?

Whether many or few, we all carry wounds from our parents. Yet we are wrong to blame them for our issues. Though we don't choose our parents, we can choose how we respond to their mistakes in raising us.

What issue in our lives do we blame on others? How can we trust God to help us move beyond our past and not be held captive by it?

[Read about Lo-Ruhamah in Hosea 1:6 and Hosea 2:23. Discover more in Romans 5:8.]

168. LO-AMMI

Lo-Ammi is the son of Gomer. Given what his name means, he is also the result of adultery, just like Lo-Ruhamah. He may have the same biological father as Lo-Ruhamah, or they may have different dads. Regardless, Hosea is not his father.

Again, it is God who gives him his name, not his mother, biological father, or stepdad. The name Lo-Ammi means *not my people*, which carries a double implication.

In a direct way, his name reminds all that Hosea is not his father. Each time Hosea calls to Lo-Ammi, he effectively says, "Come here, 'son who is not mine'."

More importantly, there is a deeper spiritual meaning, which is God's focus. In this way, Lo-Ammi personifies God's people. Because of their repeated rejection of God, he will reject them. He will disown them, saying, "You are not my people."

Yet he will only turn from them for a time. He looks forward to the day when he can change their name from "You are not my people" (that is, Lo-Ammi), to "children of the living God."

What name does God have for us as an individual? How can we better embrace the truth that as Jesus's followers we are children of the living God?

[Read about Lo-Ammi in Hosea 1:8–10 and Hosea 2:23. Discover more in 1 John 3:1.]

169. MICAH (5)

The prophet Micah is a contemporary of Isaiah. Micah's ministry overlaps and follows Hosea's. We know little else about Micah from the Bible except that he comes from Moresheth, but Scripture doesn't reveal where it is.

Micah prophesies to the nations of Israel and Judah during the reigns of several kings: Jotham, Ahaz, and Hezekiah of Judah.

He delivers strong words from God. This should convict the people, but it doesn't. Instead, they take offense. The other prophets —false prophets—tell Micah to stop talking, as if his silence will keep God's plans from happening.

Micah responds with sarcasm, saying that if a prophet proclaimed plenty of wine and beer for all, the people would flock to him. Rather than accept the truth, the people prefer to anesthetize themselves from it.

Telling the people what they want to hear—as opposed to what is true—is making a false prophecy. When the prophets don't say what the people want to hear, the people turn against them. This is a consumeristic mindset, embracing what's pleasant, even if it's wrong.

It happened to Micah. It happened to Jesus. And it still happens today.

How willing are we to share God's truth with others? How do we react when we face opposition?

[Read about Micah in Micah 1:1–2 and Micah 2:6. Discover more in Jeremiah 26:18.]

170. NAHUM (1)

F ollowing closely after Micah and Isaiah is Nahum. Nahum is an Elkoshite. He only appears once in the Bible, so we know nothing else about him from Scripture.

We do, however, know his message. He prophesies destruction against the city of Nineveh and the nation of Assyria, just like Jonah did about a century earlier. Back then the people received Jonah's lackluster message and repented.

This time the people of Nineveh do not.

We know that God used Assyria to punish Israel for them repeatedly turning away from him. This doesn't suggest Assyria is a good nation or favored by God. In his omnipotence, he uses them to accomplish what he had warned his people would happen.

Though some may think God unfair to punish Assyria for accomplishing his purpose, that's exactly what he will do. Nahum makes this clear when he declares that God opposes Nineveh, the capital of Assyria.

Just because Assyria fulfilled God's will doesn't mean it found favor with him or that he will spare the nation from punishment for the evil it did.

Is it too much of a stretch to consider that we could do God's will but still fall short of his expectations and therefore receive punishment?

We can't secure our salvation by what we do. We can't earn eternity through our behavior.

Instead, we realize salvation when we follow Jesus and believe in him to save us.

What are we doing to try to earn God's favor and salvation? Does God owe us anything when we do his will?

[Read about Nahum in Nahum 1:1. Discover more in Ephesians 2:8–9.]

171. HEZEKIAH (1)

F ive generations after Joash, his descendant Hezekiah
becomes king of Judah. He's one of the few good ones,
perhaps the best. The Bible says he trusts in the Lord God.
No king of Judah before or after him is like him. He does right like
King David. He removes the high places (which King Jehoshaphat
had left) and destroys all the elements of foreign worship, even the
bronze snake Moses had made, since the people were burning
incense to it.

Scripture says that Hezekiah follows the Law of Moses and
enjoys success in all he does.

Yet, despite this, opposition arises.

Sennacherib, the king of Assyria (recall Assyria in the chapter
about Jonah), comes with a large army, intent on capturing
Jerusalem. Overwhelmed by the size of Sennacherib's force and
discouraged by his blasphemous threats, Hezekiah seeks the Lord in
desperation, imploring him for deliverance. By miraculously deliv-
ering the people, the Almighty would prove he alone is the
Lord God.

The prophet Isaiah sends a message to Hezekiah that God will
deliver him and the people from Sennacherib's threat. That night an

angel of God kills 185,000 Assyrian soldiers. Sennacherib returns home where two of his sons assassinate him.

In this way, God delivers Hezekiah and the people of Judah from a much stronger force. The army of Judah didn't need to do a thing. God rescued them as promised.

Later, Isaiah tells the king to organize his estate, for he will soon die. Distraught, Hezekiah appeals to God in tears, asking the Almighty for a reprieve. That's when Isaiah receives an update from God, a change of plans.

God now promises that Hezekiah will recover from his near-fatal illness and live another fifteen years. Unsure what to think, Hezekiah asks Isaiah for a sign that this will happen. (This reminds us of Gideon's fleece.) Hezekiah's request makes sense because, within a short span of time, Isaiah delivered conflicting messages to the king.

To confirm that the second prophecy supersedes the first, God offers to make the sun travel backward for a time. This will be a sign to Hezekiah that his recovery will take place, just as Isaiah foretold.

The sun does indeed go back, Hezekiah gets better, and the king lives fifteen more years. After Hezekiah's recovery, he writes a psalm of praise to God.

How do we react when we receive conflicting instructions from God? Does our faith remain steady no matter what happens, or does it decrease amid uncertainty?

[Read about Hezekiah in 2 Kings 18–20. Discover more in Isaiah 38:9–22 and Matthew 1:1–10.]

172. ZEPHANIAH (1)

Following Nahum is the prophet Zephaniah. The only information the Bible gives us about Zephaniah is his parentage and that he prophesies during the reign of King Josiah. Zephaniah is the son of Cushi, grandson of Gedaliah, great-grandson of Amariah, and great-great-grandson of Hezekiah. But knowing his lineage gives us no more insight into his person.

Zephaniah's prophetic words address an array of nations, including Judah and exiled Israel, with many more countries, along with the entire world. He also has a stinging rebuke for the people's spiritual leaders, a warning which we all—leaders and laity alike—should take seriously and diligently guard against.

Despite all this, Zephaniah ends his prophecy with hope for the people. Though they live in a difficult era and the immediate future is bleak, there will come a time when God will gather his people and bring them home. He will give them honor and praise from all the inhabitants throughout the earth.

And that's something to anticipate.

When we struggle, do we focus on our present trials or look forward to a better tomorrow? Regardless of our situation, do we place our confidence in the Lord?

[Read about Zephaniah in Zephaniah 1:1. Discover more in Zephaniah 3:4 & 20.]

173. JEREMIAH (6)

Jeremiah, the son of Hilkiah, is both a prophet and a priest. The book of Jeremiah is about the life and ministry of this prophet, but Baruch compiled the content based on Jeremiah's dictation and the scribe's own chronicling of Jeremiah's life. Because of this, we know more about Jeremiah than any of the other prophets who appear in the Bible.

In reading the book of Jeremiah, we see that Jeremiah suffers much for speaking God's word to an unreceptive audience. At various times his detractors threaten him, throw him into a pit, and place him in stocks. More than once, his life is in danger. False prophets oppose and humiliate him. And though he tells the people not to flee to Egypt, they do exactly that and force him to go with them.

One thing unique to Jeremiah's prophecy is that—unlike other prophets—he gives a specific timeline to one of his pronouncements. He says the people will live in exile in Babylon for seventy years (Jeremiah 25:11–12).

Four chapters later, he adds more detail. Jeremiah says that after the seventy years of captivity have passed, God will rescue them, bring them home, and punish Babylon (Jeremiah 29:10).

In the books of Daniel and Ezra, we see this occur just as the prophet proclaimed.

How do we react when people attack and malign us for obeying God? And if we're never persecuted, what does this say about how we live our life?

[Read about Jeremiah throughout the book of Jeremiah. Discover more in 2 Chronicles 36:21–23 and Daniel 9:2.]

174. BARUCH (1)

Baruch, Jeremiah's faithful scribe and assistant, is the son of Neriah, the son of Mahseiah. Since we know nothing about these two men, they give us little insight into the life of Baruch. All we know about him is what appears in the book of Jeremiah, a document that Baruch wrote most, or all, of at Jeremiah's behest.

In addition to serving as Jeremiah's scribe, Baruch also speaks on the prophet's behalf when he cannot. This puts Baruch in the crosshairs of Jeremiah's detractors. As a result, Baruch also suffers for doing God's work.

The final time we read of Baruch in the book of Jeremiah is Jeremiah's prophetic words about his scribe. Imagine taking dictation for a man of God and then writing down what the Almighty says about *you*. This short instruction from God, through Jeremiah, to Baruch ends with the Lord's promise that wherever Baruch goes, God will let him escape with his life.

The book of Jeremiah notes that when the people flee to Egypt to avoid King Nebuchadnezzar's assaults, they drag both Jeremiah and Baruch with them. But Baruch later resurfaces in Babylon and prophesies to God's people there. In this we see the fulfillment of Jeremiah's prophecy for his scribe.

Do we think that if we're faithful to God, he will always rescue us? When faced with persecution for obeying our Lord, do we give up or persevere?

[Read about Baruch in Jeremiah 32:12–16, Jeremiah 36:4–32, Jeremiah 43:1–7, and Jeremiah 45:1–5. Discover another noteworthy scribe in Nehemiah 13:13.]

175. EZEKIEL

Ezekiel is a priest, the son of Buzi. In addition to being a priest, he's also a prophet. He lives in Babylon in exile, the result of King Nebuchadnezzar conquering Judah and deporting most of its people.

The entire book of Ezekiel is about him and by him, but aside from headings added to the Bible, Ezekiel's name only appears twice in his book and nowhere else in all of Scripture. This is because Ezekiel writes in the first person, often using the pronouns *I* and *me*. This makes his writing more personal and accessible.

Instead of using his given name, God often calls Ezekiel "son of man," which occurs ninety-three times in the book of Ezekiel.

This nickname may serve to remind Ezekiel of his humanity, despite being in the priestly line and a prophet of God. Although every one of God's priests, prophets, and servants would be in the same situation, God rarely calls anyone else *son of man*.

As such, we can see *son of man* as a name of affection that God gives his priest-turned-prophet. This suggests a close relationship between God and Ezekiel.

Ezekiel, as *son of man*, foreshadows Jesus arriving on earth as *the* Son of Man, an even greater affirmation of his close connection with God. Father God sends his son, the Son of Man, to earth to die for us and save us.

If God has a special nickname for us, what might it be? Do we have a close relationship with God, like Ezekiel?

[Read about Ezekiel throughout the book of Ezekiel. Discover another person called son of man in Daniel 8:17. Discover more about Jesus—*the* Son of God—throughout the books of Matthew, Mark, Luke, and John.]

176. OBADIAH (8)

The Bible has *nine* men with the name Obadiah, but the prophet is the best known among them. Overlapping Habakkuk and following him is Obadiah. His one-chapter book in the Bible records what God reveals to him in a vision.

He likely lives in Judah. His prophecy addresses the nation of Edom, descendants of Esau. Because he is a contemporary of Habakkuk, the prophet's ministry may occur during the reigns of Jehoiachin or Zedekiah.

Among other things, Obadiah criticizes Edom for its pride. The primary issue, however, is not what the people of Edom did but what they didn't do. When foreign armies attacked Jerusalem, they did nothing to help. They stood aloof and watched (Obadiah 1:11).

Theirs is not an act of commission, but of omission. Their sin is inaction.

In what ways are we proud today? What are our sins of inaction?

[Read about Obadiah in Obadiah 1:1. Discover more in Proverbs 16:18 and 1 John 2:16.]

177. HABAKKUK

Following Zephaniah by a few years is Habakkuk. He is the only person named Habakkuk in the Bible, and he only appears in his book of prophecy. His ministry overlaps Jeremiah's and most of Obadiah's. He prophesies just before Judah's fall to Babylon.

Unlike the other prophets' writings, however, Habakkuk's book records a dialogue between him and God, with God's response emerging as prophecy.

Habakkuk complains to God. It reads like a lament. Then God responds. Next, Habakkuk issues a second complaint. Again, God responds.

Habakkuk doesn't complain a third time. Instead, he concludes with a lengthy prayer that reads like a psalm.

We may identify with Habakkuk's grumbles to God.

His two best-known objections are in Habakkuk 1:5 and Habakkuk 2:3–4. New Testament writers quote both. Acts 13:41 references the first passage, while Romans 1:17, Galatians 3:11, and Hebrews 10:37–38 cover the second.

Yet we might do better to focus on the end of his prayer, as found in Habakkuk 3:18–19. Despite his discouragement,

Habakkuk pledges to rejoice in the Lord and express joy in God, his Savior.

May we do the same.

Though God hears our complaints, might we grumble to him too often? What can we do to better rejoice in our Lord and Savior?

[Read about Habakkuk in Habakkuk 1:1–2. Discover more in Psalm 35:9.]

DANIEL, PROPHET AND DREAM INTERPRETER

With God's people in captivity, we see him preparing for them to return to the promised land from their exile. But first we must consider Daniel. After him we'll look at the accounts of Ezra, Nehemiah, and Esther. This will wrap up our Old Testament story arc and prepare us for the arrival of Jesus in the New Testament.

178. DANIEL (2)

When King Nebuchadnezzar conquers the nation of Judah, he deports most of its citizens. He sets aside young men who are members of the royal family and nobility. They'll undergo training and be forced into a lifetime of service to the king who conquered them and killed many of their friends and relatives.

Daniel is one of these young men. He may even be a boy when this occurs.

Despite this challenging situation, Daniel and three of his friends pledge to serve God, even though they could have turned their backs on him for not protecting their nation and keeping them safe.

In his work for his captor, Daniel conducts himself well, rising to a level of power and respect. Among other things, he interprets dreams. He also serves at least four kings: Nebuchadnezzar, Belshazzar, Darius, and Cyrus. In all, Daniel's loyal service spans seventy years.

The book of Daniel opens with six stories about him and his three friends. Best known is the account of when his detractors toss him into a pit of hungry lions because of his steadfast worship of

God. God protects Daniel throughout the night. The next day he's removed and replaced by his accusers. The hungry lions devour them.

The book of Daniel ends with four prophecies. The third prophecy, as recorded in Daniel 9, happens during the reign of King Darius.

Daniel recalls Jeremiah's prophecy of seventy years of exile before the people return. The time is almost up. Daniel fasts and prays, confessing the sins of the people and imploring God to act. That's when God's prophetic word comes to his prophet. His perspective, prayer of confession, and faith in God are powerful examples for us all to follow.

The Bible says Daniel remains in Babylon until the first year of King Cyrus, and Daniel has another vision two years later.

King Cyrus also allows some of the Israelites to return home. Included in the list of those allowed to return is the brief mention of a man named Daniel (Ezra 8:2). This could be another person with the same name, or it could be this Daniel, who lived in exile for seventy years and returned home in his old age.

Are we willing to be like Daniel and confess the sins of our people? If we're forced to serve people who harmed us, as happened to Daniel, do we still give them our best?

[Read about Daniel in the book of Daniel. Discover more about Nebuchadnezzar in 2 Kings 24:1-17.]

179. SHADRACH, MESHACH, AND ABEDNEGO

When Babylon conquers Judah, Daniel and his three friends—Hananiah, Mishael, and Azariah—are seized. They're deported to Babylon. Their names may be unfamiliar to you. That's because this trio is better known by the names given to them by their captors: Shadrach, Meshach, and Abednego.

We read of Shadrach, Meshach, and Abednego only in the book of Daniel. They always appear as a trio and never as individuals. Therefore, we'll consider them as a unit, a team. Recall the wise words of King Solomon that a cord of three strands is not easily broken (Ecclesiastes 4:12).

So it is with Shadrach, Meshach, and Abednego. Together they are strong.

In Babylon, King Nebuchadnezzar erects a monument of gold and decrees that everyone should bow before it and worship the image. The punishment for failure to do this is being burned alive.

Shadrach, Meshach, and Abednego refuse to bow.

When Nebuchadnezzar confronts them, they boldly confirm that they will not worship the image. Instead, they'll stay true to their God who is able to save them from the king's fiery furnace of death. They proclaim confidence that God will rescue them, but even if he doesn't, they'll still worship him only.

Nebuchadnezzar orders that Shadrach, Meshach, and Abednego be bound and thrown into the furnace. The fire is so hot that the guards who toss them in die. Yet Shadrach, Meshach, and Abednego do not.

The king is astounded to see the three of them walking around in the furnace, unbound and unharmed. With them is a fourth man, whom Nebuchadnezzar says looks like "a son of the gods."

The king calls them to come forth. When Shadrach, Meshach, and Abednego emerge, they're unaffected by the inferno. Their hair is not singed, their robes are not seared, and they don't smell like smoke.

Amazed, Nebuchadnezzar praises their God, even though the king doesn't know who their God is. Nebuchadnezzar decrees that anyone who says a word against the God of Shadrach, Meshach, and Abednego must die.

How willing are we to die for our faith? Who can we join as a "cord of three strands" to live a strong, God-honoring life?

[Read about Shadrach, Meshach, and Abednego in Daniel 3. Discover more in Daniel 1:6–7 & 19.]

180. NEBUCHADNEZZAR

When I consider Nebuchadnezzar, the king of Babylon, I think of an evil man who killed countless people and plundered the nations he conquered. Yet, despite his many shortfalls, I wonder if God views him differently.

Jeremiah quotes the Lord as calling Nebuchadnezzar "my servant." God plans to use Nebuchadnezzar to exact judgment on the nation of Judah for their ongoing disregard for him and his commands. This is exactly what happens. Therefore, it shouldn't surprise us to see God at work in Nebuchadnezzar's life.

Here are three stories, all from the book of Daniel:

First, Nebuchadnezzar has a dream. He believes the dream has meaning, but it confounds him. He calls all the wise people in his realm to explain it to him. Yet he refuses to tell them the dream. To verify their interpretation is correct, he requires them to first tell him the dream and then clarify what it means. If they don't have the discernment to know the dream, how can he trust their explanation?

But no one can tell Nebuchadnezzar his dream.

Then Daniel comes forward, confirming that he can't either but acknowledging that God will reveal it to him. He tells the king his dream and interprets it.

Relieved, Nebuchadnezzar honors Daniel and gives him rule over the entire province of Babylon. The king affirms God as the God of gods and King of kings, one who reveals mysteries. This is quite a proclamation for a pagan ruler to make.

Our second story about Nebuchadnezzar is the one we covered in the chapter about Shadrach, Meshach, and Abednego. The king makes a giant statue for the people to worship and decrees that anyone who fails to do so will be burned to death. The trio refuses, but God delivers them from the deadly blaze unscathed.

Amazed, Nebuchadnezzar praises God and decrees that anyone who talks against God will face a gruesome death and have their house destroyed. This is quite amazing for a king who doesn't know God.

Our last story is about another dream Nebuchadnezzar has. Daniel's interpretation reveals that, because of the king's pride, he will go insane as punishment. After seven years his sanity will return, and he'll resume his rule.

Everything happens as Daniel declared.

Upon being returned to his rule, Nebuchadnezzar praises "the Most Holy God," giving him honor and glory. He pens not one, but two passages that praise God for his infinite rule and unsurpassed power. Each reads much like a psalm.

Imagine that. Nebuchadnezzar—the nemesis of God's people—praising the Lord most high through two psalms.

In these three stories, the evil King Nebuchadnezzar emerges as an enigma. Seeing how God interacts with him—and the king's response—fills me with awe and wonder.

How open are we to see God at work in people we view as wicked? If an evil king can affirm God's power, what can we do?

[Read about Nebuchadnezzar in Daniel 1:1–2 and Daniel 2–3. Discover more in 2 Kings 24–25 and Jeremiah 25:8–9.]

181. BELSHAZZAR

Belshazzar succeeds his father Nebuchadnezzar as ruler over Babylon. Once established, he throws a grand party for one thousand of his nobles. While drinking wine—perhaps too much—he orders that the goblets taken from the temple in Jerusalem be brought out to serve his guests. In doing so, they praise their gods of gold and silver, of bronze, iron, wood, and stone.

Suddenly fingers from a disembodied hand appear and write four words on the wall. Belshazzar is understandably frightened. His face turns pale, and his knees grow weak.

He must know what it says, but no one can read the words or decipher its meaning. At the suggestion of the queen, he calls for Daniel, promising grand rewards if Daniel can interpret the message.

Daniel dismisses the king's offer and instead chastises him.

Despite knowing what happened to Nebuchadnezzar when he became proud, Belshazzar repeated his father's error. He refused to humble himself.

Daniel reads the words and interprets them: "Your days are numbered. I repeat, your days are numbered. You've been judged and fall short. Your kingdom will be taken from you and given to the Medes and Persians."

That night Belshazzar is killed, and his kingdom is taken over by Darius, the Mede.

Though Nebuchadnezzar received a warning and a second chance, Belshazzar did not. This is perhaps because he should have known better.

What must we do to avoid committing the same mistakes as our parents? Though God is a God of mercy, are we wrong to assume he'll always give us a second chance?

[Read about Belshazzar in Daniel 5. Discover more in Daniel 7:1 and Daniel 8:1.]

182. DARIUS

When Darius becomes king in place of Belshazzar, he establishes a hierarchy to help him rule, with Daniel as one of three administrators overseeing 120 province governors. Daniel conducts himself so well that the king plans to set him over the entire kingdom.

The other two administrators and the province governors, however, don't want this. But they cannot find any way to discredit Daniel, for his work is beyond fault.

Instead, they seek to attack him through his beliefs and practices. They maneuver Darius into issuing a decree that, for one month, the people can only pray to him and no other. The king foolishly agrees.

Daniel disregards this new law and continues to pray to God as usual. His detractors catch him and insist the king throw Daniel into a den of hungry lions.

Darius doesn't want to, but he has no choice. He cannot change the law. He gives the order, hoping God will rescue Daniel. In the morning, he finds that this is exactly what happened, with God shutting the lions' mouths and Daniel being unharmed. He has Daniel removed from the den and his detractors thrown in instead. The lions quickly kill them.

Then this pagan ruler does something surprising. He issues another decree, that the people must fear and reverence the God of Daniel. The king praises God and exalts him.

This would have never happened had Daniel not risked his life to do what was right.

How can we protect ourselves from being maneuvered into doing something we shouldn't do? How much are we willing to risk to worship God?

[Read about Darius in Daniel 6. Discover more in Daniel 9:1 and Daniel 11:1.]

183. ZERUBBABEL

As we read the genealogy of Jesus in Matthew 1, we read many familiar names in the first eleven verses. After the nation is exiled to Babylon, we see many unfamiliar names. But one name pops out. It is Zerubbabel, whom the Bible identifies as the son of Shealtiel.

Zerubbabel is the great-grandson of Josiah, the last God-honoring king of Judah. This means that Zerubbabel has royal blood in him. He's a descendant of David and an ancestor of Jesus.

It's after Josiah's death that Nebuchadnezzar conquers Judah and deports the people. This means Zerubbabel is born in Babylonian captivity. But he gets to return to his ancestral home when King Cyrus allows the people to go back to Judah.

With Zerubbabel being part of David's line, it's not surprising for him to assume a lead role and serve as governor, even though there is no nation for him to rule as king.

Under Zerubbabel's leadership, the people restore the altar in the destroyed temple and resume sacrifices as prescribed by Moses. Zerubbabel also begins rebuilding the temple, but legal opposition arises and halts progress.

The prophet Haggai addresses this, as does the prophet

Zechariah. And even though Zechariah prophesies that Zerubbabel will complete the temple, the Bible does not confirm this. Scripture credits Ezra with rebuilding the temple (though Zerubbabel is likely present and may have been involved with it).

After Ezra completes the temple, Nehemiah rebuilds the wall around Jerusalem. But this all starts with Zerubbabel rebuilding the altar and restoring right worship.

What might God be telling us to rebuild or restore? How do we respond when we face opposition to completing what God has called us to do?

[Read about Zerubbabel in Ezra 3:2, Ezra 4:1–3, and Ezra 5:1–2. Discover more in Haggai 1–2, Zechariah 4:9–10, and Matthew 1:11–12.]

184. HAGGAI

Haggai is the first prophet to emerge after the people of Judah return home from captivity. He's also a preacher. He ministers after some Hebrew exiles in Babylon are repatriated under the decree of King Darius.

Haggai is a contemporary of Zechariah and Ezra, along with Zerubbabel. He also has a two-chapter book that contains his prophecy. It's called Haggai. Notably, the writers of Hebrews quote Haggai 2:6 in Hebrews 12:26.

Haggai chastises God's people who live in fine homes while the temple—the Almighty's home here on earth—sits in shambles.

God tries to get his people's attention for years, but they continue to miss it. Each year they plant much but harvest little. They struggle to survive.

God wants them to rebuild his temple and reestablish it as their center of worship. He wants his people to put him first and think about their own needs second. When they do this, he will provide for them.

Ezra remarks that the people prosper under the preaching of Haggai, a fine tribute to his effectiveness as God's messenger.

If we feel we aren't receiving God's blessings, it's up to us to determine why. Do we need to reorder our priorities, or do we need to allow our Lord to grow himself in us, preparing us for the future?

Is seeking God and doing his will our first priority? What do others say about our work?

[Read about Haggai in Ezra 5:1 and Ezra 6:14. Discover more in Haggai 1–2.]

185. ZECHARIAH (15)

As mentioned in the chapter on Zechariah (1), there are many men in the Bible with the name Zechariah. The main three are Zechariah (1), the king of Israel; Zechariah (15), the prophet; and Zechariah (22), the father of John the Baptist.

Zechariah (15) is the son of Berekiah and a descendant of Iddo. Just like Haggai, Zechariah is a prophet and preacher in the land of Judah after some Hebrew exiles return home under the decree of King Darius. Zechariah is also a shepherd.

Zechariah's prophecies occur in the fourteen-chapter book that bears his name. It's the longest book of all the Minor Prophets. Three New Testament writers—Matthew, Mark, and John—quote from the book of Zechariah.

Though the name Zechariah shows up in seven verses in the book of Nehemiah, which chronologically follows Ezra, these reference several other men with the same name and don't likely refer to the prophet Zechariah.

The book of Ezra covers what happens with the repatriated people, with both Zechariah and Haggai joining together in their prophecies. They also teach the people. Under their encouragement, along with the leadership of Ezra, the Hebrew people rebuild the temple.

Zerubbabel rebuilt the altar. Now the people have rebuilt the temple. What's next is rebuilding the wall around the city, which will fall to Nehemiah.

When have our words encouraged others to act? How can we build on the work of those who went before us or complete work for others to build upon?

[Read about Zechariah in Ezra 5:1 and Ezra 6:14. Discover more in Zechariah 1:1–6.]

186. CYRUS

In the chapters on Nebuchadnezzar and Darius, we see them both praising God. Not being Jewish or believing in the Almighty, their declarations surprise us. Yet there's more. King Cyrus also issues an unexpected proclamation.

God moves Cyrus's heart to allow the people of Judah—whom Nebuchadnezzar captured and relocated—to return home and rebuild the temple. He even supplies provisions for the people to complete their task.

Cyrus feels called by God—divinely appointed—to accomplish this task. In this we see a humility in Cyrus that both Nebuchadnezzar and Belshazzar lacked.

Though the people face significant opposition when they return to rebuild the temple, along with much drama, they eventually restore their house of worship.

And this wouldn't have happened without God first moving the heart of King Cyrus to act.

How is God moving in our hearts today? What is he calling us to do?

[Read about Cyrus in Ezra 1:1–6 and Ezra 6:2–18. Discover more in 2 Chronicles 36:22–23 and Isaiah 45:1–13.]

187. EZRA

E zra's ministry begins in the latter part of Daniel's life.

Chronologically, the book of Ezra follows the ending of 2 Chronicles, with 2 Chronicles 36:23 repeated in Ezra 1:2–3. Given this, as well as other clues, some Bible scholars attribute the authorship of 1 and 2 Chronicles to Ezra.

Ezra is a priest and scribe who returns from exile with Zerubbabel to rebuild the temple in Jerusalem. The first six chapters of Ezra give the history behind this momentous development, with Ezra switching to a first-person narrative in Ezra chapters 7–9 when he arrives in Jerusalem to assess the situation.

Ezra is distressed to see that some of the Jews living there have intermarried with those of other religious beliefs, contrary to the Law of Moses. This command isn't to keep the Jewish bloodline pure but to avoid distracting them from God and watering down their faith with contrary religious practices.

Ezra takes his concern to God.

Like Daniel, and later Nehemiah, Ezra prays collectively for the people, confessing their mistakes as a group. He carries their offenses on his shoulders, offering a brief glimpse of what Jesus will later do when he carries all sins, for all people, throughout all time, upon his shoulders, when he dies as the ultimate sacrifice.

Ezra prays, confesses, and weeps. This isn't a private effort, but one done in the open for all to see. In doing so, he attracts attention, and many of the people align with him to address those who disregarded God's commands by marrying outside of their faith.

This brings about repentance, followed by correction. The actions Ezra dictates to fix this problem, however, seem extreme.

The men who married foreign women must send their wives away, along with their children. But these women may not be without fault. Implicitly they have done exactly what God warned against by turning their husbands' attention from the one true God and introducing their foreign religious practices and ideals into their family life.

Although this must be a painful decision for the men who disobeyed God, the effect on their wives and children is much more disturbing. The husbands summarily send these women and their children away to fend for themselves in a society that dismisses single moms, often forcing them to struggle in poverty.

Though this doesn't seem fair, remember that sin carries consequences. Sometimes these consequences affect others.

Which of God's commands are we ignoring? How might our sins hurt others?

[Read about Ezra in Ezra 7 and 10. Discover more in Nehemiah 8.]

188. NEHEMIAH

The events of the book of Nehemiah follow the book of Ezra, with Ezra appearing in the book of Nehemiah and Nehemiah showing up in the book of Ezra. Ezra's task was rebuilding the temple in Jerusalem, whereas Nehemiah focuses on rebuilding the city walls.

Nehemiah's story begins with him in exile, serving King Artaxerxes as cupbearer. Nehemiah's brother returns from Judah and tells Nehemiah the deplorable situation in Jerusalem, with its broken walls and burned gates.

Upon hearing this, Nehemiah sits and cries. He mourns and fasts for several days. He prays to God, confessing his sins and those of his family, along with all God's people, for disobeying the laws of Moses. He ends by asking for favor with the king. Nehemiah is specific, asking God to grant him success that very day.

God, however, delays his response.

Four months later Nehemiah makes a bold appeal to the king to return to Jerusalem and rebuild the city walls. He bravely asks the king to provide resources to make this happen. The king agrees. Nehemiah returns and rebuilds the wall, though not without a bit of drama and severe opposition along the way.

Though Nehemiah led this wall-rebuilding effort with God-honoring wisdom and enjoyed a successful outcome, it all started with prayer and confession.

Do we tend to pray first and then act, or act first and then pray when things don't work out? Are there any sins we should confess for ourselves, our family, or our community?

[Read about Nehemiah in the book of Nehemiah, especially Nehemiah 2:1–9. Discover more in Ezra 2:2.]

189. SANBALLAT

As Nehemiah sets about rebuilding the wall surrounding the city of Jerusalem, he faces obstacles. These come primarily from three men who band together to oppose him and his work. They are Sanballat, Tobiah, and Geshem. Though they share a common goal to stop Nehemiah, each plays a different role in their efforts to halt the rebuilding of the wall.

First is Sanballat. He's a Horonite, which is likely a race or people group.

Sanballat heads the opposition to Nehemiah and the rebuilding of the wall. Tobiah and Geshem take their lead from Sanballat. Without his leadership, the other two men might not have had the boldness to act against Nehemiah's efforts.

We don't know Sanballat's motivation for obstructing Nehemiah's work, but we do get a hint of it when we later learn that Sanballat's daughter is married to the high priest's grandson. This marriage between a priest and a foreign woman is extra distressing because it occurs not long after Ezra's efforts to eliminate all such unholy marriages.

Perhaps through this alliance, Sanballat enjoys a bit of influence that he fears he might lose under Nehemiah's leadership. This seems a legitimate concern because Nehemiah later drives away Sanballat's son-in-law. Implicitly, this removes Sanballat's connection with the high priest and Jerusalem, lessening his ability to impact what goes on in the temple and in the city.

Have we ever opposed something with selfish motives? Do we use our position to influence God-honoring issues, the matters the Almighty cares about?

[Read about Sanballat in Nehemiah 2:10–20, Nehemiah 4:1–7, and Nehemiah 6:1–14. Discover more in Nehemiah 13:28.]

190. TOBIAH (2)

Tobiah the Ammonite is the second of three people who oppose Nehemiah's efforts to rebuild the wall. He takes his lead from Sanballat. At one point we even see Tobiah at Sanballat's side, agreeing with him and speaking against the wall as Nehemiah works to rebuild it.

Later, the pair hires Shemaiah to oppose Nehemiah and intimidate him by claiming there's a death threat against him, attempting to distract him from his work.

Tobiah's main part in the opposition to Nehemiah, however, is that he's receiving intelligence information from the nobles in Judah about Nehemiah and what he is doing. And he is in communication with them, attempting to influence them.

Whereas Sanballat heads up the opposition, we see Tobiah working behind the scenes to gather information and influence the people to advance their agenda.

Like Sanballat, Tobiah is also allied with the Jews through the marriages of both him and his son. Tobiah even has a room improperly assigned to him in the temple courts.

When Nehemiah initiates his final reforms, the people read from the Law of Moses, which says no Ammonites or Moabites can ever enter the temple (Deuteronomy 23:3). As an Ammonite, this includes Tobiah. He's out.

Have we ever let someone wrongly influence us? Have we ever worked behind the scenes to advance what is right or acted with subversive intent?

[Read about Tobiah in Nehemiah 2:10 and 6:10–19. Discover more in Nehemiah 13:4–9.]

191. GESHEM

The final member in the trio of opposition to Nehemiah is Geshem, an Arab.

Once Nehemiah finishes rebuilding the walls, but before he can set the gates, Sanballat and Geshem send Nehemiah a message, imploring him to meet with them.

Nehemiah realizes this is a ploy. He knows they want to hurt him, possibly even kill him, so he declines. Four times they send him this message, and four times he says, "No."

The fifth time, Sanballat and Geshem send Nehemiah the same message via a courier, along with an unsealed letter. In it, they accuse Nehemiah of inciting a revolution and trying to set himself up as king. Sanballat states that Geshem can confirm these charges are true.

In their desperation to stop Nehemiah, Geshem libels him, stating outright lies as truth.

What should we do when others attack our character? What is a God-honoring way to respond when people lie about us?

[Read about Geshem in Nehemiah 6:1–7. Discover more in Nehemiah 2:19.]

192. XERXES

King Xerxes is a powerful ruler, but he doesn't make wise decisions. Here are several examples:

During his reign, he celebrates his wealth and splendor for 180 days. Following this is a weeklong banquet, with an abundance of wine. On the last day, Xerxes—likely under the influence—commands Queen Vashti to come before everyone wearing her crown.

We could understand this command as to be sure to wear her crown. Yet another understanding is that it's a command to wear *only* her crown. This second interpretation would certainly explain why she refuses. Regardless, Xerxes is incensed.

The king asks his aides what to do, and they recommend he depose Vashti. He agrees.

Later, he calms down and remembers what happened. His aides propose an elaborate plan to replace Vashti. He agrees to their suggestion. Out of hundreds of women, possibly thousands, he picks Esther and makes her queen.

In this, we see Xerxes making a rash command while he was drunk. Rather than admit his error, he follows the advice of his aides to deal with the fallout by banishing Vashti. When they recommend a plan to replace her, he agrees even though this will forever negatively impact hundreds of women. But he doesn't care.

Later, Haman—the king's highest official—wants to kill Esther's Uncle Mordecai, along with the rest of the Jews. Haman maneuvers Xerxes into giving him the needed authority. Using the king's signet ring, he issues an edict to kill all the Jews and plunder their property.

Here we see Xerxes giving Haman full authority to act on his behalf. Haman issues an edict designed to cause the death of tens of thousands of Jews throughout the kingdom. But because the king fails to investigate Haman's claims, he's unaware of what's poised to happen.

Fortunately, Esther tactfully brings the situation to Xerxes's attention. Though the edict Haman issued under Xerxes's authorization is irrevocable, a new edict can offset it.

Not learning from his earlier mistake of giving Haman his signet ring, Xerxes now gives it to Mordecai, who issues an edict of his own. Though this protects the Jews from annihilation, it brings about the death of 75,000 others.

Though it's wise to seek advice, how do we know when to not follow the counsel we receive? When have we wrongly given our authority to others?

[Read about Xerxes in Esther 1, Esther 3:10–15, and Esther 8:1–14. Discover more in Daniel 9:1.]

193. VASHTI

At this point, some of God's people have returned home from exile, but not all have.

Back in Persia (formerly Babylon) the mighty King Xerxes shows off his wealth, splendor, and majesty to his people for a full 180 days, nearly half a year. Then he gives a weeklong banquet for everyone in the citadel, complete with an open bar.

At the same time, Queen Vashti gives her own celebration, a seven-day party for the women of the palace.

On day seven, an inebriated Xerxes commands the beautiful Vashti to parade herself in front of his drunken guests. The virtuous queen, however, refuses to debase herself before their ogling eyes.

Embarrassed, the enraged ruler asks his advisors what to do. Their answer is quick.

They want to keep other women from following Vashti's example of insubordination and thereby disrespecting their husbands. They fear widespread marital conflict. Therefore, they advise the king to immediately remove Vashti from her position as queen and forever ban her from being in his presence.

With little thought, the king agrees to their proposal. He issues an irrevocable edict and sends Vashti away.

Queen Vashti reacted to the king's degenerate request with chaste virtue. She refused to stoop to his drunken depravity, regardless of the cost. In doing so, she paid a heavy price for her integrity.

This is the last we hear of Vashti in Scripture.

How much value do we place on maintaining our integrity? How much will we risk to do what's right?

[Read about Vashti in Esther 1:7–20. Discover more in Esther 2:1-4.]

194. MORDECAI (2)

ordecai is a descendant of the Jews exiled by Nebuchadnezzar when he conquered Judah. Mordecai takes care of Esther, his orphaned niece. In this we see Mordecai as a man of integrity who cares for his relative. He adopts her and treats her like a daughter.

Esther is beautiful, with an attractive figure.

When King Xerxes seeks a replacement for Queen Vashti, Esther is one of the virgins rounded up in the national initiative to find a new queen.

Mordecai instructs Esther to keep her nationality and background secret. We don't know why he does so, but it may be that he fears anti-Semitism from the king's court. Mordecai does what he can to check on his adoptive daughter as she waits in the king's harem.

Around this time, the king elevates one of his advisors, Haman, to a position of high authority. Everyone kneels in honor before Haman, as the king commands, but Mordecai refuses to do so.

Though the Bible doesn't explicitly say it, we can assume Mordecai sees bowing to Haman as being disrespectful toward God, who is the only one deserving his homage.

Mordecai's refusal to bow enrages Haman. He embarks on an extreme revenge campaign, but killing just one Jew isn't enough. To get back at Mordecai, Haman plans to kill all the Jews who live throughout the nation's provinces. He wants to exterminate the entire race.

Mordecai's refusal to bow before Haman could cost him his life —and the lives of all his people.

Are we willing to honor God even if it might result in our death? Will we maintain our integrity even if it puts other people's lives in jeopardy?

[Read about Mordecai throughout Esther 2–10. Discover another man who risked his life for his faith in Daniel 6:6-23.]

195. ESTHER

After King Xerxes banishes Queen Vashti from his presence, he regrets his rash decision, his irrevocable edict. His aides suggest that he find a replacement. They round up the most beautiful virgins in the land for the king to try out (yes, it's as bad as it sounds). The most pleasing one will be crowned queen.

This isn't a voluntary beauty pageant. It's conscripted service that forces the selected women into a harem. Esther, also called Hadassah, is rounded up in the dragnet. She waits at least four years for her assigned time to spend the evening with the king.

After she sleeps with the king, he proclaims her queen.

When Haman plots the Jews' extermination, Mordecai challenges Esther, his relative and adopted daughter, to intervene with the king on the Jews' behalf. She balks. It's been a month since she's seen the king, and she risks immediate execution by appearing before him without a summons. Mordecai begs Esther to take the risk, saying, "What if God put you in your position to address this exact situation?"

Eventually she agrees. "If I die, then I die," she says.

In preparation, Esther fasts for three days and asks others to fast with her.

When she approaches the king, he spares her life. Instead of directly appealing to him, however, she invites him and Haman to a private banquet with her that night. She then requests they come a second evening. At this second dinner, she reveals Haman's plot, appealing to the king for justice.

Because of her actions, Haman is executed, and the Jews are granted the right to defend themselves and attack their enemies.

The festival of Purim celebrates Esther and her heroics in saving her people.

Though she took time to pray and fast, Esther bravely set her own safety aside and risked her life to save others.

Are we willing to work to save the lives of others even if it puts ours in jeopardy? What risks will we endure to do what's right?

[Read about Esther in Esther 2–10. Discover others who fasted and prayed in Daniel 9:3, Ezra 8:23, and Nehemiah 1:4.]

196. HEGAI

Hegai is not a well-known biblical figure. He's virtually unheard of. His name only shows up four times in Scripture, all in Esther 2. At best, most readers consider him a footnote to Esther's story. But his role may have been pivotal in her quest to find favor with the king.

Hegai, a eunuch, oversees the king's harem of virgins as they await their turn to spend the night with him. Afterward, they join the king's harem of concubines, under the direction of another eunuch.

As she awaits her turn, Esther wins the favor of Hegai. He gives her extra attention and a special place in the harem. When it's her turn to sleep with the king, she seeks Hegai's advice. We don't know what he suggests, but he must have given her wise counsel, for the next day Xerxes proclaims Esther as queen.

Though this outcome is no doubt a result of Esther's actions, let's not dismiss Hegai's role in this. God may have used his sound advice to bring about Esther's success, putting her in position for what happens next.

When people seek our counsel, do we give them the soundest advice we can? Regardless of our job, do we always do our best?

[Read about Hegai in Esther 2:3–15. Discover others who offered sound advice in Exodus 18:19 and Daniel 4:27.]

197. HAMAN

Haman is the son of Hammedatha, the Agagite, but the Bible doesn't define what an Agagite is. It could be his race, or it could be a creed he holds. Given Haman's actions, we can wonder if an Agagite is defined by anti-Semitism. Regardless of what Agagite means, we do know that Haman is, in fact, prejudiced.

As the valued advisor of King Xerxes, the king elevates Haman and commands people to kneel before him. Mordecai refuses. In retribution, Haman decides to slaughter Mordecai's entire race—all the Jews.

His plan is thwarted, however, when Esther intervenes for her people. As a result, Haman is executed, along with his ten sons.

Haman should have been pleased when the king elevated him in position and stature. He wasn't. Haman should have been pleased to have people bow in fear and reverence before him. He wasn't.

Haman shouldn't have let Mordecai's attitude disturb him, but he did. His irrational anger and lust for revenge so controlled him that it resulted in his death. In the end he lost his life, along with the position and prestige the king granted him.

When have we been unhappy with what we've had and strived for more? When have we overreacted—in thought or in deed—to a situation or circumstance?

[Read about Haman throughout Esther 3–9. Discover more about revenge in Romans 12:19 and anger in Ephesians 4:26.]

198. ZERESH

Zeresh is the wife of the anti-Semitic Haman. After Haman complains about Mordecai to his family and friends, Zeresh recommends Haman construct a seventy-five-foot pole and seek the king's permission to impale Mordecai on it. Haman delights in this idea and follows his wife's advice.

His plan is foiled, however, when the king has a different idea. Instead of hearing Haman's plan to execute his nemesis, the king commands Haman to honor Mordecai. After completing this distasteful task, the mortified Haman returns home in humiliation.

Then Zeresh predicts her husband's downfall. Since Mordecai is a Jew, she says, Haman doesn't stand a chance.

She's right.

A few days later, Haman is impaled on the same pole he constructed for Mordecai's execution. Zeresh's initial advice to her husband becomes the tool for his death.

Zeresh gave her husband the guidance he wanted to hear. What if she had counseled him differently, instead encouraging him to rise above his vendetta and not seek revenge?

When we give advice to others, do we offer them the easy answer or the right one? How can we best support our family and friends?

[Read about Zeresh in Esther 5:9–14 and Esther 6:12–14. Discover another wife who offers advice to her husband in Job 2:9.]

199. JOEL (13)

The Bible mentions fifteen men named Joel, but the prophet Joel is the best known of them all.

From Scripture, it's not possible to place him chronologically, but many Bible scholars view him as a contemporary of Malachi, possibly with overlapping ministries.

Joel addresses the exiles who have returned to Judah from Babylon. His prophecies talk more about locusts than any other prophet. Only the much longer book of Exodus contains more mentions of locusts than the book of Joel.

In the Bible, locusts usually represent widespread destruction for their ability to strip a field of all its foliage and destroy the crop. Such is the case with the locusts in Joel's prophecy.

Perhaps his best-known passage is Joel 2:28–32. In this, the prophet looks forward to the day when all God's people will receive the Holy Spirit. They will prophesy, have supernatural dreams, and see visions.

Peter quotes this passage in his Pentecost message to explain to the people gathering what is happening: Jesus's followers are not drunk. They're filled with the Holy Spirit, just as Joel foresaw (Acts 2:15–16).

How does Joel's prophecy about the Holy Spirit apply to us today? Do we embrace the Holy Spirit's power or dismiss it?

[Read about Joel in Joel 1:1. Discover more in Acts 2:15–21 and Romans 10:13, which quotes Joel 2:32.]

200. MALACHI

The name Malachi occurs only once in the Bible. The reference gives no background information about him. Bible scholars believe he is a contemporary of Joel.

Malachi addresses the exiles who have returned to Judah from Babylon. He talks about the many ways God's people fall short of the Lord's expectations.

Perhaps his most stinging rebuke is that those who do evil are falsely proclaimed as doing what is good in God's eyes. This assessment displeases the Almighty. We too often encounter this same wrong perspective today.

In a parallel passage, Isaiah proclaims woe to such people (Isaiah 5:20). We should do the same.

In what ways does our world today view those who do evil as good? How can we stand strong amid the twisting of God's truth?

[Read about Malachi in Malachi 1:1. Discover more in Luke 7:27 and Romans 9:13, which quotes Malachi 1:2–3.]

JESUS

F rom our perspective today, the purpose of the Old Testament is to point us to Jesus. Though Jesus doesn't appear by name in the Old Testament, he exists throughout its pages.

Jesus is there at creation when God said, "Let us make . . ." (Genesis 1:26; John 1:2, 10; and Colossians 1:15–17).

He is there in the supernatural encounters between God and his people, arriving as the angel of the Lord (Genesis 16:7–11 and over fifty other verses).

And Jesus appears frequently in the prophetic words of God's messengers who look forward to the future Messiah who will come and save the people (such as in Isaiah 9:6–7 and in more than four dozen other passages).

Last, we see Jesus alluded to in the closing chapter of the Old Testament. Malachi foresees the return of the prophet Elijah (Malachi 4:5–6), whom we see personified in John the Baptist (Matthew 17:10–13). John will prepare the people for Jesus's arrival, announcing that he will die for their mistakes and save them (Hebrews 10:10–14).

What a fitting way to conclude the Old Testament.

In what ways has God revealed Jesus to you through the Old Testament? What is your response?

[Read about Jesus's salvation in Luke 1:76–79, John 10:28, Acts 4:11–12, and Ephesians 2:8, as well as throughout the New Testament. Discover more about Jesus in the Old Testament in Isaiah 9:6–7.]

~

If you liked *200 Old Testament Sinners & Saints,* please leave a review online. Your review will help others discover this book and encourage them to read it too.

Thank you.

SINNERS, SAINTS, AND US

From a basic understanding, this book considers characters in the Old Testament who make mistakes (sinners) and who do good (saints). We can look at their errors to avoid their blunders or to correct our missteps. We can also look at their successes to celebrate what they did well and inspire us to do better.

A more correct understanding of sinners and saints, however, is to acknowledge we are all sinners: every one of us. This includes you and me. As such, we all fall short of God's Old Testament expectations.

Yet Jesus offers us a better way.

When we repent and follow him, he makes us right with Father God, wiping away the penalty our sins deserve and giving us a clean slate. In this way we become saints. This sainthood—our right standing with God—is a gift freely available to anyone who wants to receive it.

All we need to do is accept what Jesus offers. We don't need to change our behavior to gain God's attention or earn our salvation—we can't. It's impossible. Instead, God has prepared a no-strings-attached present that he graciously offers to us.

It's in *response* to this gift that we seek to change our behavior as a way of saying "thank you" to Jesus for the salvation he has given us.

May the Old Testament characters of the Bible inspire us to move forward as we become more Christlike in response to our salvation. Here are some questions to consider and to spur us on:

- What Bible characters inspired you the most?
- Which stories surprised you?
- What errors (sins) do you need to repent of and move away from?
- What errors (sins) must you guard against, so you don't repeat the same mistakes?
- What characteristics from these Old Testament people can you celebrate and imitate?
- What characteristics can you aspire to follow so you become more Christlike?

Contemplate your answers, and seek God to help you move forward. May he bless you as you read his Word and apply it to your life each day. May he receive your efforts as an act of worship, and may the world see your life as a powerful witness.

[Discover more in 2 Timothy 3:16–17].

DUPLICATE NAMES

Several people covered in this book share their names with other biblical characters. Sometimes these repeated names occur in the same family tree, where the name given to one child is in honor of someone in their lineage. For example, Abraham's grandfather is Nahor (1), and his brother is Nahor (2).

To avoid confusion, I've added a numerical suffix to distinguish duplicates. (Further complicating matters, some of these people also share names with cities or regions.)

Here are the names in this book which are shared with other people in the Bible. Though not always possible, I attempted to list them in chronological order, with the person we covered in italics.

Abigail

Abigail (1), sister of David (1 Chronicles 2:13–16)

Abigail (2), wife of Nabal, who later married David upon her husband's death (1 Samuel 25:39–42)

Abigail (3), daughter of Nahash and sister of Zeruiah the mother of Joab (2 Samuel 17:25)

Abimelek

Abimelek (1), a king during the time of Abraham (Genesis 20:1–2)

Abimelek (2), the son of Gideon (Jerub-Baal) (Judges 9:1)

Abimelek (3), a king during the time of King David (Psalm 34:1)

Adonijah

Adonijah (1), the fourth son of King David (2 Samuel 3:4)

Adonijah (2), a Levite during the reign of King Jehoshaphat (2 Chronicles 17:7–9)

Adonijah (3), a leader during the time of Nehemiah (Nehemiah 10:14–16)

Ahab

Ahab (1), an evil king of Israel (1 Kings 16:29–30)

Ahab (2), a lying prophet during the time of Jeremiah (Jeremiah 29:21–22)

Ahimelek

Ahimelek (1), a priest during the time of King David (1 Samuel 21:1)

Ahimelek (2), a Hittite who was in King David's army (1 Samuel 26:6)

Amasa

Amasa (1), commander over Absalom's army and later for King David (2 Samuel 17:25)

Amasa (2), a leader in Ephraim during the reign of King Ahaz (2 Chronicles 28:12)

Amnon

Amnon (1), King David's firstborn son (2 Samuel 3:2)

Amnon (2), a son of Shimon (1 Chronicles 4:20)

Amos

Amos (1), a prophet (Amos 1:1)

Amos (2), an ancestor of Jesus (Luke 3:25)

Athaliah

Athaliah (1), a son of Jeroham (1 Chronicles 8:26–27)

Athaliah (2), an evil woman who killed her royal family so she could seize the throne and become queen of Judah (2 Kings 11:1)

Athaliah (3), a family head and father of Jeshaiah who returned to Judah from exile in Babylon (Ezra 8:7)

Baruch

Baruch (1), Jeremiah's scribe and spokesman (Jeremiah 36:4–8)

Baruch (2), the son of Zabbai who rebuilt a section of the wall in Jerusalem (Nehemiah 3:20)

Baruch (3), a signatory of the people's promise (covenant) to observe the Law of Moses; he could be the same as Baruch (2) or Baruch (4), but not both (Nehemiah 10:1–6)

Baruch (4), son of Kol-Hozeh who agreed to live in Jerusalem (Nehemiah 11:3–5)

Basemath

Basemath (1), one of Esau's wives and daughter of Elon (Genesis 26:34)

Basemath (2), a daughter of Ishmael (Genesis 36:3)

Basemath (3), a daughter of Solomon and wife of Ahimaaz (1 Kings 4:15)

Benjamin

Benjamin (1), the twelfth son of Jacob and second of Rachel (Genesis 35:24)

Benjamin (2), great-grandson of Benjamin (1) (1 Chronicles 7:6–11)

Caleb

Caleb (1), son of Jephunneh, who spied out the promised land for Moses and gave a favorable report (Numbers 13:6, 30)

Caleb (2), son of Hezron (1 Chronicles 2:18)

Daniel

Daniel (1), one of King David's sons (1 Chronicles 3:1), also called Kileab (2 Samuel 3:3)

Daniel (2), a member of the royal family or nobility exiled to Babylon. He served under at least four kings: Nebuchadnezzar, Belshazzar, Darius, and Cyrus. He's best known for surviving a night in a den of lions. Though it's a stretch, he could also be Daniel (3) and/or Daniel (4) (Daniel 1:6)

Daniel (3), a family head who returned from exile with Ezra; he could be the same person as Daniel (4) (Ezra 8:1–2)

Daniel (4), a signatory of the people's promise (covenant) to observe the Law of Moses; he could be the same person as Daniel (3) (Nehemiah 10:1–6)

David

David (1), the second king of Israel, father of Solomon, and ancestor of Jesus (1 Samuel 16:13)

David (2), though this obscure reference could be to King David, given the context, he's likely a different man (Ezra 8:2)

Deborah

Deborah (1), nurse of Rebekah (Genesis 35:8)

Deborah (2), a judge and prophet (Judges 4:4)

Ehud

Ehud (1), a judge (Judges 3:15)

Ehud (2), a son of Bilhan (1 Chronicles 7:10)

Eleazar

Eleazar (1), a son of Aaron and a priest (Exodus 6:23)

Eleazar (2), a son of Abinadab, consecrated to guard the ark (1 Samuel 7:1)

Eleazar (3), a son of Dodai and one of David's mighty warriors (2 Samuel 23:9–10)

Eleazar (4), a son of Mahli (1 Chronicles 23:21)

Eleazar (5), a descendant of Parosh who returned to Judah from captivity (Ezra 10:25)

Eleazar (6), a priest during the time of Nehemiah; he *could* be the same as Eleazar (5) (Nehemiah 12:42)

Eleazar (7), an ancestor of Jesus (Matthew 1:15)

Eliezer

Eliezer (1), the lead servant of Abram (Abraham) (Genesis 15:2)

Eliezer (2), a son of Moses (Exodus 18:2–4)

Eliezer (3), a son of Beker (1 Chronicles 7:8)

Eliezer (4), a priest during the reign of King David (1 Chronicles 15:24)

Eliezer (5), a son of Zikri and tribal leader during the reign of King David (1 Chronicles 27:16)

Eliezer (6), a son of Dodavahu and prophet during the reign of King Jehoshaphat (2 Chronicles 20:37)

Eliezer (7), a leader who returned from captivity with Ezra (Ezra 8:16)

Eliezer (8), a priest guilty of marrying a foreign woman (Ezra 10:18)

Eliezer (9), a Levite guilty of marrying a foreign woman (Ezra 10:23)

Eliezer (10), a descendant of Harim guilty of marrying a foreign woman (Ezra 10:31)

Eliezer (11), an ancestor of Jesus (Luke 3:29)

Elihu

Elihu (1), son of Barakel the Buzite and friend of Job (Job 32:2)

Elihu (2), the great-grandfather of Samuel (1 Samuel 1:1–2, 19–20)

Elihu (3), brother of King David (1 Chronicles 27:18)

Elihu (4), one of King David's military leaders, from the tribe of Manasseh (1 Chronicles 12:20)

Elihu (5), a descendant of Obed-Edom and implicitly a gate-keeper for King David (1 Chronicles 26:7–8)

Elijah

Elijah (1), a son of Jeroham, likely from the tribe of Benjamin and part of King Saul's family tree (1 Chronicles 8:27)

Elijah (2), a prophet, known as Elijah the Tishbite, during the time of King Ahab (1 Kings 17:1)

Elijah (3), a priest and descendant of Harim who married a foreign wife during the time of Ezra (Ezra 10:21)

Elijah (4), a priest and descendant of Elam who married a foreign wife during the time of Ezra (Ezra 10:26)

Eliphaz

Eliphaz (1), the Temanite and friend of Job (Job 2:11)

Eliphaz (2), the son of Esau (Genesis 36:10)

Elkanah

Elkanah (1), a son of Korah (Exodus 6:24)

Elkanah (2), a son or descendant of Elkanah (1) (1 Chronicles 6:26)

Elkanah (3), another descendant of Elkanah (1) (1 Chronicles 6:27)

Elkanah (4), the husband of Hannah (1 Samuel 1:1–2)

Elkanah (5), one of King David's warriors (1 Chronicles 12:6)

Elkanah (6), doorkeeper of the ark during the reign of King David (1 Chronicles 15:23)

Elkanah (7), an official under King Ahaz (2 Chronicles 28:7)

Elkanah (8), an ancestor of Berekiah (1 Chronicles 9:16)

Enoch

Enoch (1), son of Adam and Eve's son Cain (Genesis 4:17)

Enoch (2), a descendant of Adam and Eve's son Seth and ancestor of Jesus (Genesis 5:21–24)

Er

Er (1), firstborn son of Judah and first husband to Tamar (1) (Genesis 38:1–7)

Er (2), an ancestor of Jesus (Luke 3:28)

Gad

Gad (1), the son of Jacob and Zilpah; his seventh and her first (Genesis 35:26)

Gad (2), a prophet during the reign of King David (1 Samuel 22:5)

Gershom

Gershom (1), a son of Moses (Exodus 2:22)

Gershom (2), a family head who returned to Judah with Ezra (Ezra 8:1–2)

Gomer

Gomer (1), a son of Japheth (Genesis 10:2)

Gomer (2), wife of Hosea (Hosea 1:2–3)

Hezekiah

Hezekiah (1), a king of Judah and ancestor of Jesus (2 Kings 18:1 and Matthew 1:1–10)

Hezekiah (2), the great-great-grandfather of the prophet Zephaniah (Zephaniah 1:1)

Hezekiah (3), listed among the returning exiles during the time of Ezra and Nehemiah (Ezra 2:16)

Ishmael

Ishmael (1), the son of Abraham and Hagar (Genesis 16:11)

Ishmael (2), son of Nethaniah (2 Kings 25:23–25)

Ishmael (3), son of Azel (1 Chronicles 8:38)

Ishmael (4), the father of Zebadiah (2 Chronicles 19:11)

Ishmael (5), the son of Jehohanan and a commander in Jehoiada's army (2 Chronicles 23:1)

Jehoshaphat

Jehoshaphat (1), son of Ahilud and a recorder during the time of King David (2 Samuel 8:16)

Jehoshaphat (2), one of Solomon's district governors and the son of Paruah from the tribe of Issachar (1 Kings 4:17)

Jehoshaphat (3), a king of Judah, the great-great-grandson of King Solomon, and an ancestor of Jesus (1 Kings 15:24)

Jeremiah

Jeremiah (1), a descendant of Manasseh (1 Chronicles 5:23–24)

Jeremiah (2), one of David's warriors from the tribe of Benjamin (1 Chronicles 12:2–4)

Jeremiah (3), the fifth of David's warriors from the tribe of Gad (1 Chronicles 12:10)

Jeremiah (4), the tenth of David's warriors from the tribe of Gad (1 Chronicles 12:13)

Jeremiah (5), the grandfather of King Jehoahaz (2 Kings 23:31)

Jeremiah (6), a priest and prophet, the son of Hilkiah (Jeremiah 1:1)

Jeremiah (7), a signatory of the people's promise (covenant) to observe the Law of Moses (Nehemiah 10:1–2)

Jeremiah (8), a priest or Levite who returned from exile with Zerubbabel; he could be the same person as Jeremiah (7) (Nehemiah 12:1)

Jezebel

Jezebel (1), the evil wife of King Ahab (1 Kings 19:1–2)

Jezebel (2), a self-proclaimed prophet whom Jesus criticizes in Revelation (Revelation 2:20)

Joash

Joash (1), a grandson of Judah (1 Chronicles 4:21–22)

Joash (2), a grandson of Benjamin (1 Chronicles 7:6–8)

Joash (3), father of Gideon (Judges 6:11)

Joash (4), son of Shemaah and one of King David's warriors (1 Chronicles 12:3)

Joash (5), in charge of King David's supplies of olive oil (1 Chronicles 27:28)

Joash (6), a son of King Ahab (2 Chronicles 18:25)

Joash (7), a boy king of Judah and grandson of Athaliah (2 Kings 11:2)

Joel

Joel (1), firstborn son of Samuel (1 Samuel 8:2)

Joel (2), a descendant of Simeon and clan leader (1 Chronicles 4:35–38)

Joel (3), a descendant of Reuben (1 Chronicles 5:1–4)

Joel (4), another descendant of Reuben (1 Chronicles 5:7–8)

Joel (5), a descendant of Gad (1 Chronicles 5:12)

Joel (6), ancestor of a temple musician during the reign of King David (1 Chronicles 6:33)

Joel (7), another ancestor of a temple musician during the reign of King David (1 Chronicles 6:36)

Joel (8), a descendant of Issachar and son of Izrahiah (1 Chronicles 7:1–3)

Joel (9), one of David's mighty warriors (1 Chronicles 11:38)

Joel (10), a descendant of Gershon during the reign of King David (1 Chronicles 15:7)

Joel (11), a leader over the half-tribe of Manasseh during the reign of King David (1 Chronicles 27:20)

Joel (12), a Levite during the reign of King Hezekiah (2 Chronicles 29:12)

Joel (13), the prophet (Joel 1:1)

Joel (14), a gatekeeper guilty of marrying a foreign woman (Ezra 10:43)

Joel (15), a descendant of Benjamin who settled in Jerusalem during the time of Nehemiah (Nehemiah 11:7–9)

Jonah

Jonah (1), God's unwilling prophet from Gath Hepher, the son of Amittai, who spends three days in the belly of a large fish (Jonah 1:1; 2 Kings 14:25)

Jonah (2), the father of Simon Peter (Matthew 16:17)

Jonathan

Jonathan (1), a priest, the son of Gershom (Judges 18:30)

Jonathan (2), a descendant of Judah (1 Chronicles 2:32)

Jonathan (3), son of King Saul and friend of David (1 Samuel 14:1)

Jonathan (4), one of David's mighty warriors, the son of Shagee the Hararite (1 Chronicles 11:34)

Jonathan (5), David's nephew, who killed a large man (1 Chronicles 20:6–7)

Jonathan (6), the son of Uzziah, who oversaw some of the king's storehouses (1 Chronicles 27:25)

Jonathan (7), David's uncle (1 Chronicles 27:32)

Jonathan (8), son of Abiathar the priest (1 Kings 1:42)

Joseph

Joseph (1), the eleventh son of Jacob and first for Rachel; he was sold as a slave and ended up a ruler in Egypt (Genesis 30:22–24)

Joseph (2), son of Asaph (1 Chronicles 25:2)

Joseph (3), a priest guilty of marrying a foreign wife; a descendant of Binnui (Ezra 10:38–42 and possibly Nehemiah 12:14)

Joseph (4), stepfather of Jesus (Matthew 1:16)

Joseph (5), a half-brother of Jesus (Mark 6:3)

Joseph (6) of Arimathea, a disciple of Jesus and a member of the Council; he buried Jesus (Matthew 27:57; Mark 15:43)

Joseph (7) or Barsabbas, also known as Justus (Acts 1:23)

Joseph (8), a Levite from Cyprus; the apostles call him Barnabas (Acts 4:36)

Joshua

Joshua (1), son of Nun, protégé of and successor to Moses (Exodus 24:13)

Joshua (2), son of Jozadak, and a priest (Ezra 3:2)

Joshua (3), an ancestor of Jesus (Luke 3:29)

Josiah

Josiah (1), son of King Amon and king of Judah (2 Kings 22:1)

Josiah (2), son of Zephaniah (1) (Zechariah 6:10)

Jotham

Jotham (1), son of Gideon (Jerub-Baal) (Judges 9:5)
Jotham (2), a descendant of Caleb (1 Chronicles 2:47)
Jotham (3), a king of Judah (2 Kings 15:5–7)

Korah

Korah (1), a son of Esau (Genesis 36:14)
Korah (2), a descendant of Esau, through Eliphaz (Genesis 36:15–16)
Korah (3), a great-grandson (or descendant) of Levi who opposed Moses (Numbers 16:1–6)
Korah (4), a descendant of Caleb (1 Chronicles 2:42–43)
Korah (5), a descendant of Korah (3) (1 Chronicles 9:17–19)

Lamech

Lamech (1), a descendant of Cain (Genesis 4:17–18)
Lamech (2), son of Methuselah, father of Noah, and ancestor of Jesus (Genesis 5:25–31)

Levi

Levi (1), one of Jacob's twelve sons (Genesis 29:34)
Levi (2), father of Kohath (Numbers 16:1)
Levi (3), an ancestor of Jesus, who is the father of Matthat (1) and son of Melki (Luke 3:23–24)
Levi (4), another ancestor of Jesus, who is the father of Matthat (2) and son of Simeon (Luke 3:29–30)
Levi (5), also known as Matthew and a tax collector who became a disciple of Jesus (Matthew 9:9)

Micah

Micah (1), a man in the book of Judges, though arguably not a judge (Judges 17:1)
Micah (2), a descendant of Reuben (1 Chronicles 5:1–5)
Micah (3), a great-grandson of King Saul (1 Chronicles 8:33–34)
Micah (4), a grandson of Kohath and cousin of Moses (1 Chronicles 23:12 & 20)

Micah (5), a prophet from Moresheth (Micah 1:1)

Miriam

Miriam (1), older sister of Moses and Aaron (Numbers 26:59)

Miriam (2), a child of Mered (1 Chronicles 4:17)

Mordecai

Mordecai (1), an exile who returned to Judah with Zerubbabel (Ezra 2:1–2)

Mordecai (2), Esther's cousin, who raised and adopted her after the death of her parents (Esther 2:7)

Naaman

Naaman (1), a son of Benjamin (Genesis 46:21)

Naaman (2), a descendant of Benjamin and head of one of his clans, possibly the same as Naaman (1) (Numbers 26:40)

Naaman (3), a leper and commander of the army of the king of Aram (2 Kings 5:1)

Nadab

Nadab (1), a son of Aaron (Exodus 6:23)

Nadab (2), a great-uncle of King Saul (1 Chronicles 9:35–39)

Nadab (3), son of Jeroboam and a king of Israel (1 Kings 14:19–20)

Nahor

Nahor (1), grandfather of Abram (Abraham) (Genesis 11:22–26)

Nahor (2), brother of Abram (Abraham) (Genesis 11:27)

Nahum

Nahum (1), a prophet (Nahum 1:1)

Nahum (2), an ancestor of Jesus (Luke 3:23–25)

Nathan

Nathan (1), a son of King David (2 Samuel 5:13–14)

Nathan (2), a prophet during the time of King David (2 Samuel 7:1–4)

Nathan (3), one of King David's mighty warriors (2 Samuel 23:36)

Nathan (4), a descendant of Judah and Caleb (1 Chronicles 2:36)

Nathan (5), a leader who returned from captivity with Ezra (Ezra 8:16)

Nathan (6), a man guilty of marrying a foreign woman (Ezra 10:38–39)

Noah

Noah (1), the man who built the ark (Genesis 6:8–9)

Noah (2), one of the five daughters of Zelophehad (Joshua 17:3)

Obadiah

Obadiah (1), a descendant of Issachar (1 Chronicles 7:1–3)

Obadiah (2), a warrior who defected to join David (1 Chronicles 12:8–9)

Obadiah (3), a descendant of King Saul (1 Chronicles 8:38)

Obadiah (4), a palace administrator for King Ahab and devoted believer (1 Kings 18:3–4)

Obadiah (5), an official of King Jehoshaphat (2 Chronicles 17:7)

Obadiah (6), a Levite who supervised laborers when King Josiah repaired the temple (2 Chronicles 34:12)

Obadiah (7), a descendant of King Jehoiachin (1 Chronicles 3:17–21)

Obadiah (8), a prophet (Obadiah 1:1)

Obadiah (9), a Levite, son of Shemaiah, who returns to Judah from captivity (1 Chronicles 9:14–16)

Obadiah (10), a Levite, son of Jehiel, who returns to Judah with Ezra (Ezra 8:9)

Obadiah (11), a priest under Governor Nehemiah (Nehemiah 10:1–8)

Obadiah (12), a gatekeeper who guarded the storerooms during the time of Nehemiah and Ezra (Nehemiah 12:25–26)

Obed

Obed (1), the son of Ruth and Boaz and the grandfather of King David (Ruth 4:13–17)

Obed (2), one of King David's mighty warriors (1 Chronicles 11:47)

Obed (3), a gatekeeper during the reign of King David (1 Chronicles 26:7)

Obed (4), a descendant of Judah (1 Chronicles 2:37–38)

Phinehas

Phinehas (1), a grandson of Aaron (Exodus 6:25)
Phinehas (2), a son of Eli (1 Samuel 1:3)
Phinehas (3), father of Eleazar (5) (Ezra 8:33)

Puah

Puah (1), a son of Issachar (Genesis 46:13)
Puah (2), a Hebrew midwife in Egypt (Exodus 1:15–21)

Reuel

Reuel (1), a son of Esau (Genesis 36:10)
Reuel (2), Moses's father-in-law and later called Jethro (Numbers 10:29)
Reuel (3), a descendant of Benjamin (1 Chronicles 9:7–9)

Samuel

Samuel (1), a prophet and son of Elkanah and Hannah (1 Samuel 1:20–21)
Samuel (2), grandson of Issachar (1 Chronicles 7:1–2)

Sarah

Sarah (1), the wife of Abraham and mother of Isaac (Genesis 17:19)
Sarah (2), the wife of Tobias (Tobit 3:7–18 in the Apocrypha)

Saul

Saul (1), the first king of Israel (1 Samuel 10:1)
Saul (2), a young Pharisee who initially opposed Jesus's followers

before experiencing a dramatic conversion; later called Paul (Acts 9:1–19)

Shelah

Shelah (1), a descendant of Noah's son Shem (Genesis 10:21–24)

Shelah (2), an ancestor of Abraham and of Jesus (Luke 3:35)

Shelah (3), a son of Judah (Genesis 38:1–5)

Simeon

Simeon (1), the second son of Jacob and Leah (Genesis 29:33)

Simeon (2), a righteous and devout man in Jerusalem who saw baby Jesus (Luke 2:25–35)

Simeon (3), a prophet and teacher in Antioch; also called Niger (Acts 13:1)

Sons of Korah

Sons of Korah (1), Korah (Moses's cousin) has three sons: Assir, Elkanah, and Abiasaph (Exodus 6:24)

Sons of Korah (2), psalm writers or performers during the time of King David (Psalm 42:1)

Tamar

Tamar (1), the daughter-in-law of Judah and mother of his twins (Genesis 38:6–30)

Tamar (2), sister of Absalom (2 Samuel 13:1–22)

Tamar (3), daughter of Absalom (2 Samuel 14:27)

Tobiah

Tobiah (1), someone (or the ancestor of someone) who returned to Judah from exile with Zerubbabel (Ezra 2:59–60)

Tobiah (2), an Ammonite official who opposed the rebuilding of the wall in Jerusalem (Nehemiah 2:10)

Uriah

Uriah (1), a loyal soldier of King David and first husband of

Bathsheba; known as Uriah the Hittite and one of David's mighty warriors (2 Samuel 11:3)

Uriah (2), a priest during the time of King Ahaz (2 Kings 16:10)

Uriah (3), a prophet, son of Shemaiah from Kiriath Jearim, during the time of King Jehoiakim, who had him killed (Jeremiah 26:20–23)

Uriah (4), a priest during the time of Ezra (Ezra 8:33)

Zadok

Zadok (1), a priest during the time of King David (2 Samuel 8:15–17)

Zadok (2), grandfather of King Jotham (2 Chronicles 27:1)

Zadok (3), son of Baana, who helped rebuild the fallen wall in Jerusalem (Nehemiah 3:1–4)

Zadok (4), son of Immer, who also helped rebuild the fallen wall in Jerusalem (Nehemiah 3:29)

Zadok (5), a leader of the people during the time of Governor Nehemiah, possibly Zadok (3) or (4) (Nehemiah 10:21)

Zadok (6), a scribe during the time of Governor Nehemiah, possibly Zadok (3) or (4) (Nehemiah 13:13)

Zadok (7), an ancestor of Jesus (Matthew 1:14)

Zechariah

Zechariah (1), king of Israel (2 Kings 14:29)

Zechariah (2), a descendant of Reuben (1 Chronicles 5:7–8)

Zechariah (3), the gatekeeper and son of Meshelemiah (1 Chronicles 9:21 and 1 Chronicles 26:1–2)

Zechariah (4), a descendant of Saul (1 Chronicles 9:37 and possibly 1 Chronicles 15:18)

Zechariah (5), a musician (1 Chronicles 15:20)

Zechariah (6), a priest (1 Chronicles 15:24)

Zechariah (7), a Levite during the time of King David (1 Chronicles 16:5)

Zechariah (8), another gatekeeper and son of Hosah (1 Chronicles 26:10–11)

Zechariah (9), a third gatekeeper, a wise counselor, and son of Shelemiah (1 Chronicles 26:14)

Zechariah (10), father of Iddo during the time of King David (1 Chronicles 27:21)

Zechariah (11), an official of King Jehoshaphat (2 Chronicles 17:7) and possibly his son (2 Chronicles 21:2)

Zechariah (12), son of Jehoiada the priest (2 Chronicles 24:20)

Zechariah (13), a king of Judah and grandfather of King Hezekiah (2 Chronicles 29:1)

Zechariah (14), an official of King Josiah (2 Chronicles 35:8)

Zechariah (15), the prophet and a descendant of Iddo (Ezra 5:1, the book of Zechariah, and possibly Ezra 8:3)

Zechariah (16), a priest guilty of marrying a foreign woman (Ezra 10:26)

Zechariah (17), son of Amariah and father of Uzziah (Nehemiah 11:4)

Zechariah (18), father of Joiarib and descendant of Zechariah (16) (Nehemiah 11:5)

Zechariah (19), son of Jonathan (Nehemiah 12:35)

Zechariah (20), a reliable witness and son of Jeberekiah (Isaiah 8:2)

Zechariah (21), son of Berekiah, who was murdered between the temple and the altar (Matthew 23:35)

Zechariah (22), the husband of Elizabeth and father of John the Baptist (Luke 1:5–25 and Luke 1:57–66)

[With the number of obscure mentions of Zechariah throughout the Bible—fifty-nine times in nine books—it's impossible to determine accurately how many there are, but there are many. The main ones are Zechariah (1), the king of Israel; Zechariah (15), the prophet; and Zechariah (22), the father of John the Baptist. The preceding listing is reasonable but not absolute.]

Zephaniah

Zephaniah (1), a prophet and son of Cushi (Zephaniah 1:1)

Zephaniah (2), a Levite and son of Tahath (1 Chronicles 6:36–37)

Zephaniah (3), a priest and son of Maaseiah during the time of Jeremiah (Jeremiah 29:25)

Zephaniah (4), a priest during the reign of King Zedekiah and taken captive when King Nebuchadnezzar conquered Jerusalem. He could be Zephaniah (2), Zephaniah (3), or a different Zephaniah altogether (2 Kings 25:18)

Zerah

Zerah (1), a grandson of Esau (Genesis 36:13)

Zerah (2), the father of Johab, who ruled Edom (Genesis 36:31–33)

Zerah (3), one of the twins born to Tamar (1) and Judah (Genesis 38:27–30)

Zerah (4), another descendant of Judah (Joshua 7:18)

Zerah (5), a descendant of Simeon (1 Chronicles 4:24)

Zerah (6), a descendant of Levi (1 Chronicles 6:20–21)

Zerah (7), a Cushite military leader who opposed King Asa (2 Chronicles 14:9–10)

FOR SMALL GROUPS, SUNDAY SCHOOL, AND CLASSES

200 Old Testament Sinners & Saints makes an ideal discussion guide for small groups, Sunday schools, and classrooms. In preparation for the conversation, read and think about the assigned chapters of this book each week.

When you get together, discuss the questions at the end of each chapter. The leader can either use all the questions to guide your conversation or pick some to focus on.

Before beginning your discussion, pray as a group. Ask for Holy Spirit insight and clarity.

As you contemplate each chapter's questions:

- Look for errors to correct (that is, sins to confess and avoid).
- Consider unwise behaviors and thoughts you should stop.
- Identify God-honoring actions and attitudes you can aspire to.
- Celebrate areas of success and strength to encourage yourself to persevere.

For Small Groups, Sunday School, and Classes

May God speak to you as you use this book to study his Word and grow closer to him.

IF YOU'RE NEW TO THE BIBLE

Each entry in this book contains Bible references. These can guide you if you want to learn more. If you're not familiar with the Bible, here's an overview to get you started, give some context, and minimize confusion.

First, the Bible is a collection of works written by various authors over several centuries. Think of the Bible as a diverse anthology of godly communication. It contains historical accounts, poetry, songs, letters of instruction and encouragement, messages from God sent through his representatives, and prophecies.

Most versions of the Bible have sixty-six books grouped into two sections: The Old Testament and the New Testament. The Old Testament contains thirty-nine books that precede and anticipate Jesus. The New Testament includes twenty-seven books and covers Jesus's life and the work of his followers.

The reference notations in the Bible, such as Romans 3:23, are analogous to line numbers in a Shakespearean play. They serve as a study aid. Since the Bible is much longer and more complex than a play, its reference notations are more involved.

As already mentioned, the Bible is an amalgam of books, or sections, such as Genesis, Psalms, or 1 Peter. These are the names given to them, over time, based on the piece's author, audience, or purpose.

In the 1200s, each book was divided into chapters, such as Acts 2 or Psalm 23. In the 1500s, the chapters were further subdivided into verses, such as John 3:16. Let's use this as an example.

The name of the book (John) appears first, followed by the chapter number (3), a colon, and then the verse number (16). Sometimes called a chapter-verse reference notation, this helps people quickly find a specific text regardless of their version of the Bible.

Although the goal was to place these chapter and verse divisions at logical breaks, they sometimes seem arbitrary. Therefore, it's good practice to read what precedes and follows each passage you're studying. The text before or after it may contain relevant insights into the portion you're exploring.

Here's how to look up a specific passage in the Bible based on its reference: Most Bibles contain a table of contents, which gives the page number for the beginning of each book. Start there. Locate the book you want to read, and turn to that page. Then flip forward to the chapter you want. Last, skim that chapter to locate the specific verse.

If you want to read online, enter the reference into BibleGateway.com or BibleHub.com. Also check out the YouVersion app.

Learn more about the greatest book ever written at ABibleADay.com, which provides a Bible blog, summaries of the books of the Bible, a dictionary of Bible terms, Bible reading plans, and other resources.

ABOUT PETER DEHAAN

Peter DeHaan, PhD, wants to change the world one word at a time. His books and blog posts discuss God, the Bible, and church, geared toward spiritual seekers and church dropouts. Many people feel church has let them down, and Peter seeks to encourage them as they search for a place to belong.

But he's not afraid to ask tough questions or make religious people squirm. He's not trying to be provocative. Instead, he seeks truth, even if it makes people uncomfortable. Peter urges Christians to push past the status quo and reexamine how they practice their faith in every part of their lives.

Peter earned his doctorate, awarded with high distinction, from Trinity College of the Bible and Theological Seminary. He lives with his wife in beautiful Southwest Michigan and wrangles crossword puzzles in his spare time.

A lifelong student of Scripture, Peter wrote the 1,000-page website ABibleADay.com to encourage people to explore the Bible, the greatest book ever written. His popular blog, at PeterDeHaan.com, addresses biblical Christianity to build a faith that matters.

Read his blog, receive his newsletter, and learn more at PeterDeHaan.com.

BOOKS BY PETER DEHAAN

40-Day Bible Study Series

Dear Theophilus (the Gospel of **Luke**, formerly That You May Know)

Dear Theophilus, **Acts** (formerly Tongues of Fire)

Dear Theophilus, **Isaiah** (formerly For Unto Us)

Dear Theophilus, **Minor Prophets** (formerly Return to Me)

Dear Theophilus, **Job** (formerly I Hope in Him)

Living Water (**John**)

Love Is Patient (**1 and 2 Corinthians**)

Revelation Bible Study

Love One Another (**1, 2, and 3 John**)

Run with Perseverance (**Hebrews**)

James and Jude Bible Study

Matthew Bible Study

1 & 2 Peter Bible Study

Mark Bible Study

Holiday Celebration Devotional Series

The Advent of Jesus (Advent devotional)

The Passion of Jesus (Lenten devotional)

The Victory of Jesus (Easter devotional)

The Ministry of Jesus (Ordinary Time devotional)

Bible Character Sketches Series

Women of the Bible

The Friends and Foes of Jesus

Old Testament Sinners and Saints

More Old Testament Sinners and Saints

Heroes and Heavies of the Apocrypha

Visiting Churches Series

52 Churches

The 52 Churches Workbook

More Than 52 Churches

The More Than 52 Churches Workbook

Visiting Online Church

Shopping for Church

Other Books

Jesus's Broken Church

Martin Luther's 95 Theses

The Christian Church's LGBTQ Failure

Bridging the Sacred-Secular Divide

Beyond Psalm 150

How Big Is Your Tent?

Be the first to hear about Peter's new books and receive updates at PeterDeHaan.com/updates.